A Journey Back to Yourself
Find the Leader in You

Become a Master in the Game of Life

Jennifer E. Rhule

I dedicate this book to my two wonderful children, Robyn and Joel. Thank you for bringing so much love and joy into my life.

Contents

Introduction 1

In Pursuit of Happiness...21

    Exercise: Heart-Centred Listening...................30

The Power of Love..35

    Exercise: Attuning to the Power of Love...........41

    To Be in Love..42

    Be Still 44

The Sweat Lodge..45

Love Is the Answer to Freedom............................57

    Exercise: Making a Connection with Your Soul 62

    Shine 64

Our Beliefs Shape Our World 65

    There Is Scarcity 70

    How to Release Yourself from the Belief of
    Scarcity 78

    Life Is about Winners and Losers......................79

    We Are Disconnected and Separate 85

    Power and Domination Gives Us Freedom 90

    We Are Disempowered and Others Are
    Responsible...93

    Exercise Making a Difference 94

    What If: The Power of Beliefs 101

Finding Your Chosen Path....................................103

    Exercise Who Am I ? 111

Bringing Good Things to Life 121

Becoming the Conductor 127

Becoming GREAT 131

Your Journey Towards Greatness 137
Generosity..138
Action Steps: Generosity...............................140
Relationships..141
Action Steps: Relationships 144
Expansion 145
Action Steps: Expansion 148
Appreciation 150
Action Steps: Appreciation............................151
Trust 153
Action Steps: Trust..156
Ascension and Your Role 159
Make the Most of the Gift of the Present.........161
Be in Love 162
Be Wise 163
Be a Great Human Being................................163
Expand Your Awareness.................................164
Be Great in Your Work 164
About the Book...169

A Brief Word

My motivation, for writing this book is that I care deeply about the world we live in and I want to contribute in any way I can to the evolution of humanity and the creation of a sustainable future, one where we all experience love, joy, and happiness.

Having worked as a human resources and organisation development executive for nearly three decades, I have discovered that contrary to what is often said, people have an amazing capacity to embrace and lead change. People are more than capable of changing when they are the masters of their own destiny. So why is it often said that people don't like change and that change is difficult? First look at the person who has made this statement, they are usually the individual or group that are trying to impose change on another person. If a person feels part of something that they believe in and understand and when they feel they can make a difference; guess what happens, they make a difference!

The only thing in this world that is constant is change, as physical beings, our physical bodies are changing every moment .It is true when they say, change is the only constant. However, I have witnessed people becoming so overwhelmed by the demands of life that they lose their way and fail to tap into the unlimited potential that they possess.

This book is your guide—to reconnecting to your personal power, your power within, so that you are able to live a rich and fulfilling life, irrespective of what is going on around you.

When you find the leader in you and develop your mastery you will be a harbinger of transformation for good in your life and the world around you.

There is no doubt, that the demands in life are increasing, it is essential to our well-being, our community and the planet that we discover our leadership and true potential. When you find the leader in you, you will be able to navigate through what you currently experience as chaos or the increasing stresses and demands on your life with clarity and purpose in a way that your life experience is one which is both energising and fulfilling.

Introduction

We have entered what many call the *planetary phase*, a time in history when we have the means to examine the trajectory of progress from a global perspective. We can evaluate and consider the long-term and universal impact of our decisions and make informed choices about the quality of the future we create and the legacy we leave behind for future generations. We have the potential to create a social and environmentally sustainable future. The question is, do you care enough? If you do, are you willing to take responsibility and play your part?

If you care and believe that you can make difference, you can find the courage to do just that. You will discover, (if you are not aware already) that your thoughts, actions and emotions contribute to the creation of what you experience in your life and ultimately what we create in our world.

Now is the time for you to examine your life; it's time to take stock of where you are now and where you are heading. If you are dissatisfied with what you discover, it is up to each of us to make informed conscious choices which will contribute to creating the type world that we want to be part of.

If we look at our collective achievements as a civilisation, we have made many technological, medical, and scientific advances. We have sent the *Curiosity and Opportunity* rover to the surface of Mars, found cures for many life-threatening diseases, and through the Internet, revolutionised the way we work, play, and communicate.

All these achievements are noteworthy accomplishments that we should celebrate. However, when you look at the state of the world from a humanitarian, social and ecological perspective, there is clear evidence that we are falling short. Alongside these admirable technological and scientific advances, we continue to live in a world where;

- The number of unemployed youth was estimated to be 73.3 million in 2014. It is also concerning to note that the youth unemployment rate exceeded 20 per cent in two-thirds of the European countries in 2014

- In 2013, as many as 169 million youth were working but living on less than US$2 per day. The number increases to 286 million if the near poor are included, when the measure of below US$4 per day is applied[1].

- 350 million people are affected by depression and over 800, 000 people die due to suicide every year. Suicide is the second leading cause of death in 15-29-year-olds[2]

- 795 million people of the 7.3 billion people in the world, or one in nine, were suffering from chronic undernourishment.[3]

- Close to one-fifth of all children under the age of five remain undernourished, and some 860 million people continue to live in slums. [4]

- In 2015, over 200 million people remain unemployed worldwide. [5]

- 663 million people -1 in 10 - lack access to safe water 6 (World Health

[1] http://www.ilo.org/global/lang--en/index.htm 27th May 2014
[22] (Depression (World Health Organisation, 2015)Fact sheet N°369, October 2015
[3] The United Nations Food and Agriculture Organization (2015 World Hunger and Poverty Facts and Statistics, 2015) 5/12/2015
[4]http://pubdocs.worldbank.org/pubdocs/publicdoc/2015/10/5030014440582245 97/Global-Monitoring-Report-2015.pdf
[5] www.ilo.org/global/about-the-ilo/newsroom/news/WCMS_412014/lang--en/index.htm 08 October 2015
[6]Organization and UNICEF Joint Monitoring Programme (JMP). (2015))

- 2.4 billion people - 1 in 3 - lack access to a toilet.

- The estimated number of conflict-affected residents 172 million. [7]

- The economic impact of violence on the global economy in 2014 was substantial and is estimated at US$14.3 trillion or 13.4 per cent of world GDP. This is equivalent to the combined economies of Brazil, Canada, France, Germany, Spain and the United Kingdom. [8]

- Only about 25 percent of the countries in the world, primarily high-income countries, have managed to grow economically while simultaneously decreasing their environmental externalities. Even fewer have managed to delink carbon emissions from growth, challenging the world's ability to contain the impacts of future climate change to agreed-upon levels of acceptability.[9]

- 1 in 4 of the world's mammals, 1 in 8 birds, 1 in 5 sharks, 1 in 4 coniferous trees, and 1 in 3

---

[7]http://www.worldhunger.org/articles/Learn/world%20hunger%20facts%202020 02.htm Source: FAO et al, 2014b pp 8-12.
[8]http://www.visionofhumanity.org/#/page/indexes/global-peace-index

[9]http://pubdocs.worldbank.org/pubdocs/publicdoc/2015/10/5030014440582245 97/Global-Monitoring-Report-2015.pdf

amphibians are now threatened with extinction in the near future due to human activities, species are disappearing around the world faster than ever before – breaking down the life support system upon which we all depend. Reduced biodiversity means millions of people face a future where food supplies are more vulnerable to pests and disease, and where fresh water is in irregular or short supply. [10]

It could also be said that we have a leadership crisis:

- Brazil's state-run oil company, Petrobras has taken a $2bn (£1.3bn) charge for costs related to corruption [11]
- In 2008 the world experienced the worse financial crisis. It is estimated that the cost of mopping up this event has come to $11.9 trillion (£7.12 trillion), enough to finance a £1,779 hand out for every man, woman and child on the planet.[12] Despite the terrible consequences of the crash, the conduct of many

[10] http://wwf.panda.org/5/12/15
[11] http://www.bbc.co.uk/news/business-32422875

[12]http://www.telegraph.co.uk/finance/newsbysector/banksandfinance/5995810/IMF-puts-total-cost-of-crisis-at-7.1-trillion.html / Conway 10:01PM BST 08 Aug 2009 31/12/2015.

of our financial institutions continues to fall short. In 2014 and 2015 the Financial Conduct Authority, one of the bodies which is responsible for regulating the financial services industry in the UK has imposed the following fines;

- Banking group Barclays £72 million for poor handling of financial crime risks. The FCA specifically found that Barclays: Senior management at the relevant time failed to oversee adequately Barclays' handling of the financial crime risks associated with the Business Relationship and that it was unclear which senior managers were in charge of doing so.[13]

- £117m to Lloyds Bank Plc, Bank of Scotland Plc and Black Horse Ltd (together Lloyds) for failing to treat their customers fairly when handling Payment Protection Insurance (PPI) complaints Royal Bank of Scotland Plc, ("RBS") National Westminster Bank Plc ("NatWest") and Ulster Bank Ltd ("Ulster Bank") (the "Banks") £42 million for IT failures which occurred in June 2012 and meant that the

---

[13]http://www.fca.org.uk/news/fca-fines-barclays-72-million-for-poor-handling-of-financial-crime-risks 26/11/15

Banks' customers could not access banking services.[14]

- £1,114,918,000 ($1.7 billion) on five banks for failing to control business practices in their foreign exchange (FX) trading operations: Citibank N.A. £225,575,000 ($358 million), HSBC Bank Plc £216,363,000 ($343 million), JPMorgan Chase Bank N.A. £222,166,000 ($352 million), The Royal Bank of Scotland Plc £217,000,000 ($344 million) and UBS AG £233,814,000 ($371 million)

- Deutsche Bank AG (Deutsche Bank) £227 million ($340 million) for LIBOR and EURIBOR-related (collectively known as IBOR) misconduct. The fine was so large because Deutsche Bank also misled the regulator, which could have hampered its investigation. It was reported that " one division at Deutsche Bank had a culture of generating profits without proper regard to the integrity of the market. This wasn't limited to a few individuals but, on certain desks, it appeared deeply ingrained."

---

[14] http://www.fca.org.uk/news/fca-fines-rbs-natwest-and-ulster-bank-ltd-42m-for-it-failures 20/ 11/15

- Bank of America's Merrill Lynch International £13.3 million ($20 million) for failing to report transactions correctly. [15]
- Toshiba Corporation is in turmoil as a result of its $1.2 billion accounting scandal, caused by top executives setting unrealistic profit targets. The electronics company admitted to inflating its earnings over a seven-year period by close to a whopping $2 billion. [16]
- Tesco (the Uk's largest retailer) was branded 'leaderless' by suppliers following accounting scandal.
- The £250m accounting scandal that has engulfed Tesco has left Britain's largest retailer unable to run its commercial operations properly and has created a culture of fear among its buyers, according to suppliers
- "The confidence at Tesco is catastrophic. There's no leadership and those in charge know nothing about Tesco.[17]

---

[15] http://www.valuewalk.com/2015/04/bank-of-america-fined-20m-for-inaccurate-reporting/ 26.12.15 12.36pm

[16] http://www.bloomberg.com/Dave McCombs / July 21, 2015 — 3:38 AM BST /26/12/15

[17] http://www.bbc.co.uk/news/business-32026738 Simon Neville Thursday 16 October 2014/ 26/06/2016

- The UN has accused the Vatican of "systematically" adopting policies allowing priests to sexually abuse thousands of children.[18]
- FIFA, soccer's international governing body, has been plagued by institutional corruption. U.S. investigators brought charges against the organization, accusing FIFA officials of taking millions of dollars in bribes to influence clothing sponsorship contracts, the FIFA presidential election, and the selection process for the World Cup.[19]
- Exxon Mobil deliberately misleads the public about climate change. Exxon had teams of scientists studying global warming in the Arctic. The scientists concluded that global warming is real, and that it posed potential dangers for the company--higher sea levels could damage Exxon's drilling platforms, processing plants, pump stations, and pipelines. But company documents reveal that, instead of helping to combat the environmental risk, Exxon (now Exxon

---

[18] http://www.bbc.co.uk/news/world-europe-25757218/ 11/04/2014/07/07/16
[19] http://www.inc.com/will-yakowicz/biggest-big-business-fails-of-2015.html/ 26/06/16

Mobile) decided to launch a multimillion-dollar campaign questioning climate change in order to bolster company profits[20]

It is clearly evident that corruption and leadership failings are not limited to financial Services , corporations covering a wide range of industries appear to be led my individuals who have lost their moral and ethical compass.

The Securities and Exchange Commission (The US regulator) frequently find it necessary to charge corporations due to non-compliant business practices, some examples include;

- BHP Billiton (global resources company) with violating the Foreign Corrupt Practices Act (FCPA) when it sponsored foreign government officials as guests at the 2008 Summer Olympics in Beijing.[21]
- Deloitte & Touche LLP with violating auditor independence rules when its consulting affiliate maintained a business relationship with a trustee serving on the boards and audit

---

[20] http://www.inc.com/will-yakowicz/biggest-big-business-fails-of-2015.html/ Published on: Dec 23, 2015/ By Will Yakowicz 31/12/15

[21] http://www.reuters.com/June 3, 2015

committees of three funds it audited. Deloitte agreed to pay more than $1 million to settle the charges. [22]
- J.P. Morgan were ordered to pay $267 Million for Disclosure Failures Washington D.C., Dec. 18, 2015 [23]
- A China-Based Company and CEO was fined $55.6 Million for Inaccurate Disclosures
- Royal Dutch Shell was fined $48m (£29.4m) in civil and criminal fines over its contractor's involvement in bribing Nigerian customs officials. [24]
- The federal government ordered Citibank to pay $700 million to customers it said had been overcharged by the bank. The Consumer Financial Protection Bureau also ordered the bank to pay $35 million in penalties associated to the overcharging and for the bank's use of "deceptive marketing" techniques.[25]

---

[22]http://www.sec.gov/news/pressrelease/2015-137.html

[23] http://www.sec.gov/news/pressrelease/2015-283.html

[24]http://www.telegraph.co.uk/finance/newsbysector/energy/oilandgas/8111277/Shell-to-pay-48m-Nigerian-bribe-fine.html/ By Rowena Mason and Richard Blackden 8:49PM GMT 04 Nov 2010

[25] Wattles July 22, 2015: 11:35 AM ET http://money.cnn.com/2015/07/21/news/companies/citibank-fined-700m/index.html

- The Environmental Protection Agency caught Volkswagen in a huge scandal that reportedly could cost the company as much as $87 billion. VW has admitted to cheating the tests deliberately and revealed that 11 million cars worldwide were fitted with the so-called "defeat device[26]."
- Failure of HBOS linked to "colossal failure of senior management and the Board", says Banking Commission[27]
- HBOS was referred to the bank that couldn't say no, the report lays bare reckless risk and leadership failures, and attacks board for trying to blame failure on 2008 crash [28]
- Goldman bankers get rich betting on food prices as millions starve, the Bank was criticised for making £250m after destructive spikes in global food market Christine Haigh of the WDM said: "While nearly a billion people go hungry, Goldman Sachs bankers are feeding their own bonuses by betting on the price of

[26] http://www.inc.com/will-yakowicz/biggest-big-business-fails-of-2015.html

[27] http://www.parliament.uk/business/committees/committees-a-z/joint-select/professional-standards-in-the-banking-industry/news/an-accident-waiting-to-happen-the-failure-of-hbos/05 April 2013

[28]http://www.theguardian.com/business/2013/apr/05/hbos-bank-that-couldnt-say-no

food. Financial speculation is fuelling food price spikes and Goldman Sachs is the No 1 culprit."[29]

- Prosecutors investigate Vatican Bank mafia link , Anti Mafia prosecutors have asked the secretive Vatican Bank to disclose details of an account held by a priest in connection with a money laundering and fraud investigation [30]
- Morgan Stanley was fined $8.8m over prearranged trading scandal settlement[31]
- Anti Mafia prosecutors have asked the secretive Vatican Bank to disclose details of an account held by a priest in connection with a money laundering and fraud investigation. Telegraph, 10 June 2012.

You may question why I have referenced all of these facts. Well my purpose is to illustrate the extent of our leadership challenge.

[29] (Bawden | Sunday 20 January

2013 | http://www.independent.co.uk/news/business/news/goldman-bankers-get-rich-betting-on-food-prices-as-millions-starve-8459207.html

[30] http://www.telegraph.co.uk/news/worldnews/europe/vaticancityandholysee/9323288/Prosecutors-investigate-Vatican-Bank-mafia-link.htmlSaturday 26 December 2015
[31] (BBR Staff Writer Published 23 December 2015 http://www.banking-business-review.com/news/morgan-stanley-to-pay-88m-over-prearranged-trading-scandal-settlement-231215-4761410)

The consequences of corrupt or poor leadership are far reaching; the loss in reputation has an impact on the everyday lives of many people, for e.g. Scandal-hit Toshiba warns of £3bn loss and plans to cut 6,800 jobs in its consumer division. [32]

The global financial crisis that has shaken the world economy since late 2007 has impacted the lives of many individuals and families beyond imagination. It has been reported that the youth have been particularly hit hard by the crisis. Long-term unemployment has risen significantly, which is concerning as long spells of unemployment contribute to skills erosion.

Millions of people are estimated to have fallen into, or are trapped in, extreme poverty because of the crisis. The rates of mental illness, substance abuse, and suicides has increased since the onset of the crisis according to the United Nations. [33]

[32] Published: 21:55, 21 December 2015 Updated: 21:55, 21 December 2015 /3369389/Scandal-hit-Toshiba-warns-3bn-loss-amid-plans-cut-6-800-jobs-consumer-electronics-businesses.html#ixzz3vSw5t64Y
[33]
wds.worldbank.org/external/default/WDSContentServer/IW3P/IB/2013/11/14/ 000158349_20131114113429/Rendered/PDF/WPS6703.pdfTHE SOCIAL IMPACT OF FINANCIAL Otker-Robe, Inci; Podpiera, Anca Maria; Country: World;

Most of the decisions that have been made are in pursuit of generating profits, some may view this as value creation, however when we consider the systemic consequences of such decisions, it is clear to see that the negative impact is far reaching, affecting lives in ways that undermine the fabric of society.

There is no doubt, we do have a leadership crisis; Politicians have been found wanting, breaking the laws they have put in place to govern society. Decisions made by members of our financial institutions have led to global financial collapse. The morality of religious institutions is being called into question and millions of people have lost their livelihood and have been exploited by business leaders who prioritise profit above people, purpose, and meaning. But the biggest leadership crisis we have is with ourselves, if we regard ourselves as victims or powerless. Nothing could be more further from the truth. You will learn more about this later on.

If we look at our world today, our humanity trails behind our technological and scientific advances. The facts presented here speak for themselves,

Date Stored: 2013/11/14 CRISES: EVIDENCE FROM THE GLOBAL FINANCIAL CRISI Inci Ötker-Robe and Anca Maria Podpiera 2 these are just a few examples of what is occuring Through the internet, whistle blowers and alternative media channels, we are learning more about the state of our world. So be inquisitive explore what is out there, find out what resonates with you, you have the ability to discern what is true if you engage in the process of inquiry with an open heart.

Where are we heading? and where are you heading? Is the quality of your life being enriched or diminished?

If you are not affected now, you will be in the future, because ultimately everything and everyone is connected.

It is clearly evident that our current way is not producing the type of results that contribute to improving the quality of our life , building a sustainable future for all members of our global society. If wealth is a determinant in the quality of life we can enjoy, there is a definite imbalance.

In 2014, Oxfam International released a report called, "Working for the Few," that contains some startling statistics on what it calls the "growing tide of inequality."

The report states:

- Almost half of the world's wealth is now owned by just one percent of the population.
- The wealth of the one percent richest people in the world amounts to $110 trillion. That's 65 times the total wealth of the bottom half of the world's population.
- The bottom half of the world's population owns the same as the richest 85 people in the world.
- Seven out of ten people live in countries where economic inequality has increased in the last 30 years.
- The richest one percent increased their share of income in 24 out of 26 countries for which we have data between 1980 and 2012.
- In the US, the wealthiest one percent captured 95 percent of post-financial crisis growth since 2009, while the bottom 90 percent became poorer

If we continue to inflict damage to our environment at the same pace that we have in the last fifty years, the earth will not be able to provide us with resources we require to sustain human life on this planet.

It is time for us to find another way.

The change that is needed requires that we all play our part in the transformation. For eons, we have given the responsibility of leadership to someone else, we have handed over our power to others to make choices on our behalf. Why is this the case? Very often it is because we believe that we do not have the power to influence what is going on around us, that we are helpless. If we continue to hold this view, individually and collectively, it is very unlikely that the situation will improve. Standing on the side line and complaining about things will not change a thing. If we care about ourselves, our family, our community and our planet, abdication of responsibility is no longer an option. Neither is mediocrity. We all need to raise our game, I can assure you that we all have the capability to do this, there are no limitations when you discover your true power and join with others to pursue something that benefits not only you, but also others. This can be achieved when you to find the leader in you.

That is the premise of this book. When you discover your true potential and choose to live in harmony with the desires that serve your best interest, your life will be transformed for the good of yourself and humanity.

Finding your leadership is a metamorphic process, your personal transformation. To progress, you are required to let go of any ideas and beliefs that prevent you from reaching your full potential and to invite those that do.

By selecting this book, you have decided to embark on journey back to yourself.

All that is required at this stage is to open your mind and, more importantly, to open your heart. Be willing to challenge your deeply held views if you discover that they do not serve your highest purpose.

Throughout the book you will be asked to reflect upon the ideas presented. At certain points you will be asked to pause or to complete an exercise. These are important timeouts, tapping into your full potential is an active process, not a passive one. It's what you do that makes the difference.

There also are blank spaces throughout the book for you to make notes, use this as a journal to capture your thoughts, questions, and insights.

Some of the content of this book may sound farfetched, but new, different ideas always do. So I urge you engage in the process and allow your truth to emerge.

The journey of a thousand miles begins with one step.

—Lao Tzu

In Pursuit of Happiness

How much happiness do you need to be happy?

On the surface, what appears to makes us happy is very specific to each of us. Some people relate happiness to fame or achievement or the accumulation of material assets.

What if I was to say that you don't need any of these things to be happy?

Most of us go through life associating the feeling of happiness with something material but happiness doesn't need to be this way. In fact, this can be an expensive and exhausting route to happiness. When we seek happiness through things that are external to us, the feeling quickly wanes and is often short lived, and consequently we find ourselves searching for happiness over and over again.

You have the power to decide right here, right now, whether you are happy or not. This is an indication of how powerful you truly are.

Stop for a moment and recall a time when you felt really happy and in the flow of life, very often such times are associated with having an uplifting emotional experience where the feeling of love and connection with something greater than ourselves played a major part. Take a moment to recreate the happiness you felt, if you were successful in this brief exercise, you just reconnected to energy of love. I would like to point out at this stage, that whatever your experience from conducting this exercise, know that what you felt and your reaction was created by you, either consciously or unconsciously.

Happiness, like all other emotions, is in your control, you are the master. No one else can or thing can make you feel happy, only you can decide that. This truth is key to you finding your unlimited potential, nobody else can be responsible for how you feel and how you react to a situation.

When you tune into your full potential, you become a conscious creator and master of your emotions, and the conductor of your life.

If we look at our lives today, many of us find ourselves caught up in a vicious cycle, swept along by a wave of emotions. For some, life can often feel like a rollercoaster of highs and lows. Sometimes we are able to ride the waves and other times we feel crushed by them. Obtaining a sense of balance and inner peace with ourselves and challenging situations can be difficult, but it is possible.

Believe me, you can become the game master of your life, think about that for a moment and make a note of your reaction to what you have just read.

Reflection / insights

My role as the author of this book is to help you reconnect to your true essence, so that you are able to live a life that is aligned with your deepest desires and the very best of who you are.

You may find that some of what you read contradicts your current beliefs and perceptions. If that is your experience, then I have achieved my goal, because that is exactly the purpose of this book. If what you read rings true, then see this as a confirmation of what you have always known. As you embark on this journey and complete the exercises you will discover your truth. You will able to discern the veracity of what is presented to you when you listen with all of your intelligence; your heart, your mind, your body and your soul. Be open. If your mind is made up and your heart is closed, none of what you read or what you experience will resonate with your true self.

It is said that the route to discovering our true essence is through the heart, this is where we are able to tap into our true wisdom. It is the access point to your higher intelligence and ultimate power.

The Institute of HeartMath has conducted extensive research for more than twenty years about the function of the heart, they have made some significant discoveries:

During the 1960s and '70s pioneer physiologists John and Beatrice Lacey conducted research that showed the heart actually communicates with the brain in ways that greatly affect how we perceive and react to the world around us. Furthermore, in 1991, a pioneer neurocardiologist Dr. J. Andrew Armour introduced the term "heart brain." He said the heart possessed a complex and intrinsic nervous system that is a brain.[34]

The Institute of HeartMath research has also discovered the following:

- The heart sends us emotional and intuitive signals to help govern our lives.

- The heart directs and aligns many systems in the body so that they can function in harmony with one another.

- The heart is in constant communication with the brain. The heart's intrinsic brain and nervous system relay information back to the brain in the cranium, creating a two-way communication system between heart and brain.

- The heart makes many of its own decisions.

- The heart starts beating in the unborn fetus before the brain has been formed, a process scientists call "autorhythmic."

---

[34] Mc Craty, Atkinson,Tomasino,2001

- Humans form an emotional brain long before a rational one.[35]

They also reported this conclusion:

- From our research at the Institute of HeartMath, we've concluded that intelligence and intuition are heightened when we learn to listen more deeply to our own heart. It's through learning how to decipher messages we receive from our heart that we gain the keen perception needed to effectively manage our emotions in the midst of life's challenges. The more we learn to listen to and follow our heart intelligence, the more educated, balanced and coherent our emotions become. Without the guiding influence of the heart we easily fall prey to reactive emotions such as insecurity, anger, fear and blame as well as other energy-draining reactions and behaviors. "

Based on these findings, it would be wise to become more "heart led" in our lives.

You may find listening to your heart difficult to start with. It will require some perseverance, but it

---

[35] Institute of HeartMath, 2012

will be worth the effort. This process is all about building a heart-based relationship with yourself. It takes time and effort to build any relationship, and building a relationship with yourself through your heart is no exception. The more you listen to your heart, the more your relationship will flourish and grow, and you will gain full access to all your intelligence.

There is another point worth mentioning at this stage. As you read this book, you may have a sense of déjà vu. The reason for this is that the knowledge we are presenting here is knowledge that you already possess. This book is design to help you remember, to reboot your hard drive, so to speak, in the same way that we reboot a computer.

When you were born you arrived equipped with the operating system that is needed to optimise all your human software (your potential). However, during the course of life we unconsciously pick up what I will refer to as emotional and mind *viruses*, things that are external to us that impede our ability to achieve alignment with the best of ourselves. We know when a virus affects us physically, but how conscious of you of the viruses that affect your thoughts and emotions? Very often, because we lack awareness, we allow these types of viruses to attach themselves to our operating system, so to speak. In doing so, they alter the way we function, just like they do in a computer. We become infected by them and they affect what we think, what we feel and what we experience, just like a virus affects a computer.

When viruses in computers are allowed to proliferate they reduce the computer's capability to function as intended. The same applies to us: when we allow external events to define us, we inadvertently give permission for something that is external to us (the virus) to influence and change affect us. The net result is that we perform at suboptimal level.

By reading this book and completing the time-outs you have chosen to press your personal Control, Alt, delete , like you do on a computer when things are not working the way they should on your computer. its an opportunity for you to look at what is going on, you have the opportunity to examine your internal processing and the programmes that are running, so that you can make a choice about which programmes you should run, clean up or delete. The aim is to remove the things in your life that you have collected along the way, the things that have taken you off course and preventing you from performing at your best.

The path to realising your full potential is to live a heart-led life. Your heart is the portal to your soul, the part of you that is never seen but always present, and the part of you that is eternal.

This may sound far-fetched for some people. If what you have just read has awakened the sceptic in you, wait a minute! I did say that some of the ideas presented in this book would challenge your current beliefs, so let's check out what you have just read by listening to your heart has to say.

Exercise: Heart-Centred Listening

Here are the steps:

- Tune into your heart. Do this by taking at least five deep breaths (of equal depth) and directing your attention to your heart.
- Do this until you feel you have made a connection with your heart and then guide your thoughts and attention to your heart (at this stage you may choose to close your eyes).
- Focus your attention within.
- Ask the question from the centre of your heart.

  o What is my soul?

  o What does my soul desire?

Wait a few moments and listen to your heart for the answer.

An alternative to the above exercise is to take a walk in nature; observe the trees, listen to the birds, examine the flowers or blades of grass. When you feel relaxed, take a few deep breaths and ask the questions.

You may find this exercise difficult to do at first, but don't give up, focus on your breathing , allow whatever comes into your mind to come and then let it go, then ask the questions until you get an answer. You will know when you have the answers that that you need.

Make a note of your experience below:

What did you experience?

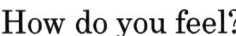

How do you feel?

What have you discovered?

If you have allowed your heart and not just your mind to respond, you will be inspired to continue your journey and discover how to live in harmony with who you truly are.

When you allow yourself to be guided by your soul purpose, you open the door to your unlimited potential and your infinite power.

The exercises in this book are milestones on your journey, they provide opportunities for you to integrate and connect with your mind, heart and your soul. Your soul is the place where all the most important questions concerning your life and your reason for being will be answered. The truth is we have the ability to find the answers, but first, you need to ask the right questions.

Each of us have an important role in the evolution of humanity, and it is imperative that we all step up to the plate and play our part. By finding yourself, you will find your leadership and you will be fully equipped with what you need to make a positive difference in your life.

If you think you are too small to make a difference, try sleeping with a mosquito.

—Dali Lama

Throughout history, ordinary people have found the capacity to shift the trajectory of our civilisation to something better. They were people like you and me, with one difference—they were not limited by their thoughts, beliefs or fear they were able to bounce back after a setback. They discovered that they were more than meets the eye. They were able to achieve extraordinary things because they had found their leadership, their primary source of potential and infinite wisdom and more importantly, they made a choice to use their potential for good. Their contribution is remembered because they improved the lives of others. I can assure you that all these people accomplished great things because they found their leadership. Now is the time to find yours.

The Power of Love

I have worked in the world of business all of my career. I have held leadership and executive leadership positions for more than thirty years, and during this time I have gained some amazing insights about life and leadership. I am now wise enough to realise that our quality of life, what we create and achieve, is determined by ourselves and what I call, our personal leadership. This has nothing to do with job title, position or status. It more about your essence, intentions and your actions.

I attained my first leadership position very early on in my life. At that time, I was working part time at a well-known fast food chain whilst completing my studies. Very soon after joining I was identified as a person who had leadership potential. I attended the company leadership university programme, and I was duly promoted. I loved my job; managing and leading others came naturally to me, because I love people and nothing gives me more pleasure than seeing a person flourish and growth and come into their own. I was only nineteen at the time, full of energy, ambition, and drive. I was inexperienced in life and lacked the maturity and confidence that I have today. As a young leader, I can see that my style was managerial and controlling. I was demanding of others, and my primary motivation was to do whatever was needed to succeed. I didn't give much consideration to whether I was being fair or reasonable to my colleagues. The only thing that mattered was delivering the results that were expected by my superiors. During this time in my career I believed that this was the best way to achieve results (I am amazed that this style of managing others is still prevalent today).

Everything was going well, but I then I experienced my first wakeup call. I had spent the day visiting members of my family. I recall it was a beautiful summer's day. After getting home, something told me to pop into work. When I got there, I could sense that something was wrong. It was a bank holiday weekend. Devon, my boyfriend, and four of his friends decided to have a boys' weekend away. I was told that Devon had been involved in a car accident, and I needed to go to the local police station to get more details. When I arrived, the police told me that my boyfriend and three of our friends had been fatally injured in a car accident. Initially I didn't comprehend what they had told me. I didn't hear the word "fatally". All I heard was that he had been injured, so I asked what his injuries were.

The police looked very perplexed. They replied, "I'm sorry, his injuries were fatal."

It took some time for me to absorb the severity of what I had been told. It was hard for me accept that the person I loved, the person that I had wished " bon voyage " only two days ago, had died. This experience shook me to the core. It was at this juncture that I started to ask questions about the meaning of life. I had a deep desire to learn and discover what life and death was all about. I wanted to understand why four young men who were in their prime of life had gone.

I was the first to be notified of Devon's passing. Devon's parents had yet to be informed, and it was clear to me that I was to be the one to tell them. The incident was to be featured in the national news because of number of fatalities and the fact that no other cars were involved. I was really concerned for Devon's parents, and I didn't want them to learn that their son had died from the news or the police. In that moment, I decided that I would take the responsibility for telling them, and I told the police that I would go to their home immediately.

I realised now that this was my first experience of leadership. I was willing to take responsibility and perform a difficult task because I really cared about how the message was delivered to Devon's parents. This was unlike the leadership I had practised until then. This heart-breaking experience helped me discover the unifying power of love and compassion. You see when you really care and have a genuine compassion for others, you discover that we are all connected through the power of love. I had no idea what I was going to say or how I was going to say it. I was hurting, but I knew that Devon's parents would hurt just as much as me and probably even more. I managed to find the inner strength to tell them, with love and compassion. The shock and pain of this experience was so profound it obliterated my ego and opened my heart. In that moment I became aligned with what I now know is true self. It was from this place that I found the power and wisdom to do what was needed.

We all have the capacity to be loving and compassionate. I discovered that when we show love, we give others the permission to do the same. I also learnt from this experience that when we live with love in our hearts, there are no regrets. My last words to Devon were an expression of love. When we parted we felt good about life, ourselves, and each other. This helped me quickly traverse the grieving process and appreciate the good times we had together. Just imagine how I would have felt if the last time I had seen him alive, we'd had an argument and parted on bad terms. I would have been full of guilt and remorse. What I have come to realise is that relationships present the greatest opportunity for us to evolve individually and collectively. When we are able to love unconditionally, irrespective of what has happened, our consciousness starts to ascend.

This whole experience fundamentally changed my perspective on life, my views on leadership, and most importantly my leadership practice. Since this time, love has been my guiding light. Admittedly, it has not been *switched on* in every moment, but the important thing is that I try to live my life consciously and I know where to find the switch.

Whenever I give talk on the subject of leadership, I always say that the heart of leadership is love. When you love yourself, love what do, and love others, there is no limit to what you can achieve.

This is the truth: Love is the creative energy source that brings good things to life. Love sustains us and connects us. It is the universal code that we all carry. Being "in love" is the key that unifies you with creation and it will keep you on the path to discovering your full potential.

Accepting this truth is essential to travelling the journey back to yourself and finding the leader in you. Our metamorphosis and transformation is complete when we are able to embrace the intelligent and liberating power of love.

It's time for another timeout. The exercise below will help you become attuned to the power of love.

Exercise: Attuning to the Power of Love

- Take five deep breaths.
- Direct all your thoughts the centre of your heart.
- Then imagine a bright light just above the top of your head, draw down the light and place it in your heart, continue to breathe deeply, direct all of your attention to your heart.
- Invite the energy love to enter through the light that is radiating in your heart
- Ask the question: What is love?
- Listen to the answer and record below what comes to mind.

When you are able to tune in to the energy of love, you unify with all that is.

Through stillness we can discover this part of ourselves. After periods of stillness, I often become inspired to write poetry. On the next few pages I have included two poems that I have written that convey the energy and power of love.

To Be in Love

When in love, no problem is too great.

When in love, we see challenging situations as opportunities to show up at our best.

When in love, we find our inner wisdom and courage to follow our dreams and what resides in our heart

When in love, there are no limitations or boundaries, everything is possible.

When in love, we believe and trust what is.

When in love, we think not of ourselves but others.

When in love, we aim to give, not receive.

When in love, the joy of giving grows, and there is no limit to what we can give.

When in love, our energy is recharged the moment we think of others.

No matter how far we search what paths we take, we soon come to realise that love is all there is.

Love is life, life is love.

Life's journey may be smooth or it may be
rough. It may consist of highs and lows.

But when in love, we find ourselves and discover
the beauty of who we truly are.

Be Still

Take time to be still,

Connect with your true self, that is love

Be still and discover the eternal energy of your
being, what you have always been and will always
be

This is the part of you that is not touched by
emotion, whether it be negative or positive, in this
place nothing exists but it contains everything

In stillness there is no pain, no time, no regrets,

no limitations, no thoughts

In this sacred place there is unity, just unity and
love, the place that you truly are

It is in this stillness that you will discover your
true beauty and magnificence, your wisdom,
intelligence and the miracle of creation, and the life
force that fuels the sun, provides the water, guides
the wind and nurtures the earth

The Sweat Lodge

The sweat lodge utilizes all powers of the universe: earth, and things that grow from the earth; water; fire; and air.

—Lakota elder Black Elk

I have explored many avenues to help me discover and develop my potential. In 2002, I decided participate in a Vision Quest. This was a key milestone in my life journey. In preparation for my quest, I completed my first sweat lodge, an ancient purification ceremony.

The sweat lodge is sacred process. The aim of the ceremony is to purify one's mind, body, spirit.

The experience is an intense one. It creates an opportunity to let go of those parts of you that do not serve your true purpose. The only way you are able to survive the extreme heat that is created within the sweat lodge is to surrender and let go of fear. Fear is an emotion that is generated by the ego. The ego is all about the protection and survival of our physical body, so its ultimate purpose is to protect us from death. In life, if we are not mindful, our egos can develop a power of their own. We can become fearful of things that are no real danger to us. We just think they are. This usually occurs when we are pushed to the edge of our comfort zone and familiarity. Our mind and ego usually establishes a frame around the world that leads us to think that there is a limit to our power and what we can achieve.

The sweat lodge is designed to simulate the process of death and rebirth. It is dark and intensely hot. Temperatures can reach 80–100 degrees centigrade. It provided an opportunity for me to glimpse my inner strength and to push past feelings of anxiety, fear, and panic. I was able transcend my ego-created limitations. As the heat increased, my mind told me that I was going to die. In truth, a part of me did – my ego. When I surrendered to the moment and let go of the fear, I discovered that I had the potential to complete the ceremony, and that is what I did. What I learnt from the whole experience is that fear limits what we can achieve.

The sweat lodge was preparation for the vision quest, which was due to start the following week. The purpose of the vision quest is to gain answers to fundamental questions:

- Who am I?
- What am I doing here?
- What is the meaning of my existence?

Its aim is to gain spiritual guidance regarding what direction to take in life and to discover one's life purpose. I learnt that all the preparation associated with the vision quest is symbolic; what you pack represents the extent to which you are attached to your current way of living and what you are prepared to leave behind and your willingness to be open and face the unknown. The weight of your pack is said to represent your "karma" and the burdens that you are carrying. I had packed my bag before leaving the UK. Although I tried to be selective, I had packed a very heavy bag, even though my intention was not to do so. But I thought it contained everything I needed for my survival.

Prior to spending the time in solitude, you venture out into sacred space, "your place of power", that will be your home during the threshold time. Needless to say, I left my heavy bag behind when I went out to find my spot.

I chose a location that was some distance from base camp. It involved quite a steep hike, and it was plus 30 degrees centigrade. I soon realised that I would have to seriously reconsider what I would take with me on my quest. If I didn't, it was doubtful that I would have been able to return to my selected spot, because in addition to my bag, I also had to transport six gallons of water! When I returned to base camp, I decided that I didn't need all of the things that I had packed. I had to reassess the balance between security and freedom. It became clear to me that holding on to the past in the form of my possessions would limit what I would experience in the present and my future.

My chosen spot and place of power was under a large old conjoined tree. For me, this represented my birth and what the vision quest meant to me. I wanted to reconnect with myself and the part of me that I had become separated from at birth. I was a twin. My brother and I were very premature. Having been born after just six months of gestation, we were very small. I was three pounds, and my twin brother was only two. Unfortunately, my twin brother died after a few days. He just wasn't strong enough to survive. The truth was that we had spent more time together in the womb than we had outside it. As I walked on the mountain to find my spot, I felt that the tree was a good representation of the union that my brother and I had. On another level, the tree represented the unity that I was seeking within myself.

The vision quest was in Mount Shasta, located in Northern California. I later learnt that this has been a place of sacred pilgrimage for people from all over the world. It is considered a revered place of great mysteries and legends. We had spent two days at base camp in preparation. prior to crossing the threshold. I was riddled with fear and apprehension (my ego). I was venturing into the unknown and petrified at the thought of spending the next four days and three nights in solitude, in the desert, with only water as sustenance. Somehow, I found the energy to overcome the fear and step into what is called sacred space and time. I just knew that this was something that I was called to do.

At the break of dawn, we completed our final preparation and I started my return to journey to the place that I had chosen. Although this was my third trip, it was no less arduous. It was August, the sun was rising, and the heat started to radiate from the ground. As I progressed, although exhausted, I started to feel a deep connection with nature and mother earth. Eventually I reached what was to be my home for the next four days. I was free from all the distractions of modern-day life, to my surprise, after what seemed like a very short time, I felt at ease. In this place of stillness, I was able to tune into the frequency of life and all that is. Each morning I was greeted by a bird chorus, and at around tea time (I didn't know the exact time, because I wasn't wearing a watch), chipmunks would appear and come very close. I felt a deep sense of unity with nature and creation.

On the second morning after I had listened to the bird chorus, a woodpecker turned up, and it was such a joy to see it pecking away at the tree across from me. On the third day, after the chipmunks finished their play day, a scorpion walked across my sleeping bag. I knew I had reached a point of unity, because I wasn't frightened. I just became the observer and realised that the scorpion needed the shade the same way I did. It had no intention of harming me.

There was no light pollution, so at night I was able to witness the beauty of the milky way and feel a deep connection with all of existence. I realised that we can only discover our potential and our connection when we go beyond the limits of the ego. This is the part of us that must die if we are to find ourselves.

Despite my initial apprehension, I thoroughly enjoyed the experience. I felt liberated and connected. It was one of the most amazing revealing and informative experience of my life. I draw on what learnt during my vision quest whenever I am faced with new and difficult challenges. I now trust my ability and know that I have a reservoir of potential that I can access whenever I need to. I am now able to put new situations into perspective, most are not life threatening, this realisation means that I am no longer fearful. When I started out on my quest and entered the unknown with very little resources to survive, I ventured beyond the edge of my comfort zone, where to my surprise, I found courage, wisdom, peace, and tranquillity.

The ultimate aim of the quest is to seek out your vision and to hear your medicine name. It is said that "once you are given your name, you will realise that all along you have been becoming this name – all along you have been becoming what you have always been." [36] My medicine name was "Raven Song". When I shared this with the group on my return, a chorus of birds began to sing !

When returned home, I researched the what the raven symbolised in ancient native traditions. I found this explanation on the Internet:

---

[36] Foster, Little , 1984

51

" Ravens bear magic and mysticism, and have a long history of myth enshrouding them. Shamans know the power of an unexpected piercing sound in shifting consciousness. Ravens have this power, giving out varied sounds, and can assist us in shifting our consciousness into various dimensional realms. Hence this is a reason why the raven is referred to as a shape shifter with magical powers. 'Raven people' can expect continual changes and spiritual awakenings throughout their lifetime.

Some native tribes refer to them as the 'keeper of secrets'. They are linked to the void, where universal secrets are kept. Obviously, their black colour is the colour linked to darkness, the place where unconscious fear resides. Ravens are master magicians and represent transformational energy, revealing to us how to rid ourselves of our inner fears. Raven will show you how to go within in yourself, into the dark areas and then illuminate them, making you 'sparkle' and bringing out your true self. Inner conflicts should then be resolved, however long buried they are – this is the deepest healing.

If raven has flown into your life, then magic and healing abound. Raven awakens the energy of magic, linking it to our will and intention. With Raven, you have the ability to make great changes in your life – now is the time when you can take the thought and make it reality. Raven knows the mystery of life, they are strongly linked with death and rebirth. Remember not to be fearful of Raven, rather give thanks for the teachings he brings. Raven chooses its student according to their knowledge. They usually stay as long as needed to help transmute karma, returning you to the light. They will lead you into the discovery of your multidimensional self and reunite you with the secrets of the multidimensional universe.[37]

This book and the *Ascent vision* is my raven's song. My vision quest helped me to connect to my leadership power in a deep and profound way. I am not advocating that the only way to find the leader in you is to participate in a sweat lodge or vision quest. Instead, I have written this book to assist in you on your journey. My vision quest inspired me to write "Ascent", which is the vision I hold in my heart for humanity, our community and our planet.

---

[37]   http://www.shamanicjourney.com/raven-power-animal-master-magician-keeper-of-secrets/ 26/06/16

Ascent: A Vision for Humanity

Ascension of humanity and

Society to a higher level of

Consciousness and a new paradigm that

Empowers and inspires individuals and
communities to create a

New way, leading to

Transformation and a world order based on unity,
love, abundance, and prosperity that is in harmony
with our environment

During my time in solitude, I gained many insights
that are conveyed in this poem.

From the Threshold

I have never been alone or devoid of love.

The greatest place to be is to be alive.

I am ready to fulfil my responsibility as a member of humanity.

It is time to move forward, to take the higher ground.

The creator and the arms of Mother Nature keep me safe and sound.

The creatures that surround me send me love, joy, and happiness.

Tomorrow I become a new and release my time till now.

I rejoice because I have discovered my courage, wisdom and connection I am one with the almighty source of unconditional and eternal love.

All my fear has gone away I am not called to act alone

Through love, compassion and our relationships we can change the world for good.

Love Is the Answer to Freedom

You may ask, if love is the answer, why is life and the world the way it is?

As I mentioned earlier, thoughts and feelings are the most powerful aspect of our being when they are charged with negative ideas, that is what is produced.

We create and experience whatever we give attention to. Think about this for a moment, where do you direct most of your attention? How do you feel most of the time?

How does your answer to these two questions influence your life?

Today, in our modern culture, so much of our energy is consumed by what is going on around us, it is so easy to get caught up in activity, and we and pay little attention to our inner world. When we constantly direct our attention outward, we move further away from our source. This is where love, our true essence and leadership power can be found. Lots of people think that they are limited to the physical, they don't believe that they are more than they can see. When you are able to tune into your true being, its similar to tuning into your favourite radio station, the frequency is ever present, all you need to do is turn the dial. When you tune in to all of your being, you access the full and true nature and your unlimited potential.

Your transformation requires that you focus your attention within so that you can increase your level of awareness. This will lead to each of us operating at higher level of consciousness. We all need to take ownership for the world we create for ourselves and how we shape and influence the world for others.

It is important to accept that we do shape and influence the world around us by the very nature of who we are. Research by the Institute of HeartMath has found that our heart produces an electromagnetic field that radiates several feet around our body. The research suggests that this field is also carrier of information. Have you ever experienced walking into a room of people and sensing the tension, or walked into a company and felt that there was a good vibe and atmosphere? What you are sensing is the frequency of the field that is created by human interactions.

This is similar to the way that the Internet transmits and connects information using electromagnetic communication. We trust that our email will arrive in the designated mailbox, even though we cannot see the Wi-Fi.

"Everything in life is vibration."

Albert Einstein

We all have our own frequency, this is determined by our, physical, emotional and mental state, our combined frequency creates what is called the *nooshere*, a collective field of human consciousness. The noosphere characterizes mind and consciousness as a unitary phenomenon. This means that the quality and nature of our individual and collective thoughts directly effects the noosphere and creates the quality of our environment—the biosphere.[38] . The way I see it is that the internet is a technological version of human consciousness.

This theory is the basis of research that is being conducted by the Global Coherence Project. They have placed a number random number generators around the world to examine whether synchronised

---

[38] http://lawoftime.org/noosphere.html 27/06/15 21.20pm

human consciousness has an influence on random systems.

The hypothesis is that there will be structure in what should be random data, associated with major global events. The study, which has been running for fifteen years, collects data network from physical random number generators located in seventy sites around the world. They are designed to randomly produce unpredictable sequences of zeros and ones. The results of the study indicate that when the feelings of millions of people become aligned due to a global event, the network of random number generators produce zeros and ones that have a structure. In others words, the random numbers become less random. Each generator is independent and should not show any relationship at all to any of the others." But when a great event synchronizes the feelings of millions of people, our network of RNGs becomes subtly structured. The probability is less than one in a billion that the effect is due to chance. The evidence suggests an emerging noosphere, or the unifying field of consciousness described by sages in all cultures [39]

---

[39]Roger Nelson 1999-2015, Global Consciousness Project

In addition, an initial conclusion from the research project is,

...that the effects we see influenced by factors that are familiar from human psychology. For example, the effects are larger in proportion to the importance of the events we examine, and they are larger if the level of emotional involvement is high. We see stronger effects when events embody or evoke deep feelings of compassion, but smaller effects when the level of fear is high. That last point seems counterintuitive to many, but upon consideration, the relationships make sense and they bear strong implications for us. Compassion is an interpersonal, connecting emotion, while fear drives us toward personal survival; it separates us.

The bottom line is that something associated with mass consciousness is changing the physical world, our network of physical random number generators. [39]

There are of course many who question and challenge the findings of this research because it does not fit readily into existing scientific models, it is at odds with existing beliefs. The study has not reached the point where everything can be explained, but there are clear indications from this research, that

"Large scale group consciousness has effects in the physical world. Knowing this, we can intentionally work toward a brighter, more conscious future."

One thing is certain, the quality of life that we live is determined by the choices we make. If we allow ourselves to be influenced negative emotions, that is what we will experience. Our perceptions of the world shape and create our world. So it is essential that you develop perceptions that serve your best interest, in doing so your efforts will impact the whole in a positive way. If you continue to allow your external world to rule your life, you will never find peace. You can only live a fulfilling and happy life when you become aligned with your deepest desires, the desires that reside in your soul.

Exercise: Making a Connection with Your Soul

The way to access your soul is through the portal of your heart.

- Check this out by becoming heart centred and the repeating the same exercise as before.
- Imagine a bright light just above the top of your head. Draw down the light

and place it in your heart continue to breathe deeply. Increase the attention to your heart.

- Invite love to enter your heart through the light.
- Ask the question: What is my soul purpose?

Listen to the answer, record below what comes to mind.

In addition to my vision quest, another memorable experience was when I participated in an art therapy session. Again this process is about letting go and freeing yourself from your ego and being in the flow. This is a creative process that enables you express your true being. The good thing is that you don't need to have any special artist talent. The art form that you create is more a free expression.

During the session I was inspired to create a painting that resembled a radiant sun containing all the colours of the rainbow. In the centre was what resembled a white light. After completing the painting, I held a moment of silence and listened deeply to my heart and to record whatever came in that moment of silence. Here is the message that came to me through as I observed my painting.

Shine

The light and core cannot be bounded

Shine out

Radiate

Be one with all eternal

Let nature ground you because she is universal

Shine, be love, in love, for love

Let there be no darkness where you enter

Be one

Find the passion, the fire within to move forward on your journey

Like the sun set you will rise and fall, but you are always eternal

Love can transform all

Trust be all colours to all

Now is the time for you to shine. We all have the ability to find peace and real happiness; however, this will be realised only when your mission is directed at living in a meaningful way and bringing good things to life.

Our Beliefs Shape Our World

Beliefs: acceptance by the mind that something is true or real, often underpinned by an emotional or spiritual sense of certainty.

Beliefs are powerful; they guide our actions and determine how we live our lives. Some of our beliefs are formed by our parents, some through our formal education or religious education, and others through our own volition. Beliefs play an important role, because they determine how we perceive and view the world.

Jha(2005) reported on the work of Peter Halligan, a psychologist at Cardiff University, who states that "Belief has been a most powerful component of human nature that has somewhat been neglected ... but it has been capitalised on by marketing agents, politics and religion for the best part of two millennia." Halligan is also reported to say beliefs are the mental architecture of how we interpret the world.

Beliefs, once established, are often difficult to change. We use them as an automatic sorting device, and through selective attention we reinforce our view of things. I'm sure you have met people who hold very fixed views on everything. This is clear evidence that their beliefs have become an established and entrenched part of their world view and the only basis of their reality. We all know how difficult it is for a person to consider an alternative after they have made up their mind. The same applies to society at large. We have developed a collective set of beliefs that limits our ability to take on board new ideas. Certain beliefs have become so entrenched in our society that they are considered true, but really they are a set of commonly shared perceptions.

How conscious are you about the beliefs that pervade society today and how they influence your life? How often do you reflect on your beliefs and examine how they play out in your life and the world?

As humans, we have the capacity to change our minds; however, to achieve this we need to increase our awareness. We need to be inquisitive and stay alert by asking questions of ourselves and the world around us. It is only when we become conscious of something that we can change it. Increasing our level of consciousness is an essential part of the transformation and change, and this is necessary part of finding your leadership.

I have an inquisitive personality. I love asking myself questions as a way of increasing my understanding of life and the world. One of the questions I often ask is how can we create a better world? I have pondered this question for a considerable time. Many answers have come to mind, but the one that resonated with my heart was that we need to change our beliefs, because it through our beliefs that we create our reality and our world!

It is often said that people do not like change; however, in my experience, this is a misconception. The truth is that people do not like *change that is imposed upon them*. Most of us are more than willing to make changes when we can see that the benefits of the change outweigh the status quo. When we develop a different point of view, a new perception, change can occur in the moment.

When we allow ourselves to be open to new possibilities, we increase our capacity to evolve. This can be achieved when you allow your mind and ego to be the observer and not the controller, when we do, we can release ourselves from the grip of fear.

Take some time to consider what usually stops you from trying something new or developing a new perspective. The two that usually appear at the top of the list are fear and what you believe. Remember, creating a new reality is just a thought away! When we build a relationship with our heart, and use this to connect with our mind and soul, we gain access the totality of who we are. This is the path to becoming enlightened and free from the limitations of the mind and become connected to the unlimited potential of life and fuelled by the power of love.

Have you ever experienced that *aha!* moment ? An inspired thought or idea that pops into your head when you least expect it, you may be in the shower or walking in nature. Have you ever asked where these pearls of wisdom come from and why they just pop into your head? And why they come to light when they do?

Great insights come to us when we are at ease and are "out of our mind". The mind is a wonderful instrument for finding solutions to problems that are similar to what you have experienced in the past. We can just download the solution from our memory bank. However, downloading old solutions when facing new challenges is less effective in these changing times. When you allow your mind and ego to step aside, you allow your ultimate intelligence to shine through. These sparks of genius are a flitting glimpse of your true capability. Increasing your level of consciousness and living a heart-led life will enable you to find and sustain your inner spark, the source of universal power and wisdom.

The rate of change in the world has been exponential in recent times. There are clear signs that our current approach individually and collectively is just not delivering the best results for humanity. The challenges that we face cannot be solved by implementing solutions that have worked in the past. Holding on to the past is a sure way of hindering your personal growth and the progress of humanity. Embarking on the journey back to yourself you will develop confidence in your ability and discover that novel solutions to the challenges you face are just a heartbeat away.

The significant problems we have cannot be solved at the same level of thinking with which we created them.

—Albert Einstein

My insight on the power of beliefs prompted me reflect on how certain beliefs play out in society and the extent to which they have become part of our prevailing culture and collective consciousness. Here are a few of the prevailing beliefs that shape our world and govern how we live our lives.

- There is scarcity
- Life is about winners and losers
- We are disconnected and separate
- Power and domination gives us freedom
- We are disempowered and others are responsible

It's now time to explore how these beliefs influence our perception of the world and our behaviour.

There Is Scarcity

The belief of scarcity underpins our current economic system. When we live through the lens of scarcity, we feel compelled to acquire and accumulate whatever we feel is or may become scarce. Scarcity, in essence, is the engine fuel of our global economic system which is dependent on the consumption of goods and services.

The strongly ingrained belief of scarcity often leads to selfish and self-centred behaviour. When the drive to accumulate becomes excessive, the seed of greed is planted. Greed is described as "an excessive desire to possess more than one needs or deserves, especially with respect to material wealth an excessive desire for more of something (as money) than is needed. [40]

Andrew Lo a professor at MIT states that" Greed occurs when the natural human impulse to collect and consume useful resources, like food, material wealth, or fame, overwhelms the constraints that maintain the social ties in a group. In other words, the accumulation of wealth becomes more important than human relationships.[41]

Accumulation like anything else, can become additive. When people become addicted, they narrow their perspective and their judgement is impaired This, to my mind, explains why top executives are able to make their employees redundant at the same time that they award themselves bonuses and pay increases. Scarcity and greed starve us of compassion and concern for others.

---

[40] *Merriam-Webster.com*, 2013
[41] Fox, 2010

The belief that there is not enough (scarcity) is a powerful force in our world today. It does not only concern material things. Time is one of the commodities that we think is in short supply. This often leads to an obsessive use of time, as we try to cram each moment of our life with an activity and we never switch off. How often have you said or heard, "I'm so busy. I just don't have time" or "I just don't have time to think." Everyone in the world today seems be short of time and stressed because of it.

Scarcity robs us of our freedom to enjoy and appreciate life in the moment. We can become so focussed on what we need tomorrow, we forget to acknowledge and appreciate what we have today.

When people believe there is not enough, they can become self-centred and act without any concern for others. I have also witnessed in my career many instances of individuals compromising their principles and integrity as a way to secure their employment. With the threat of redundancy and unemployment being at an all-time high, this type of behaviour is becoming even more prevalent.

Scarcity is constantly used to drive consumption of goods and services. We feel an urge to buy anything that has been discounted or in short supply. The belief that there is not enough is an established part of our psyche. I'm sure you have witnessed panic buying during the sale season, and when there is even a slight prospect of adverse weather conditions, it is as though we have been programmed to react is a certain way if there is a possibility that there is not enough, the fear of not having enough is a predominant force in the world today. It is so entrenched that many people are no longer conscious or aware of what is driving our feelings emotions or behaviour.

The thing that we have been led to believe is in the shortest supply is money. When I look our world today, the fear of not having enough money is the thing that enslaves us the most. It seems to be the root of most of our fears. The austerity measures that have been put in place in response to current economic climate crisis continue to reinforce this belief, amplifying the feeling of fear and insecurity on a global scale. The consequences can be seen all around us.

The truth is there is more money in circulation than ever before. The BBC reported in December 2015 that the Bank of England created £375bn ($550bn) of new money in its QE programme between 2009 and 2012, and that between 2008 and 2015, the US Federal Reserve created $3.7

trillion. The eurozone began its programme of QE in January 2015 and has so far pumped in $600bn of extra money, Originally the programme was set to run until September 2016, but it has now been extended until at least March 2017.[42]

So why do we still believe there is not enough money in the world? Maybe it's because this would undermine the fundamental principles of the current economic system which is built on the principle of scarcity. Maybe it is because of the inequitable distribution of wealth that exists in the world, because those who possess the most are gripped by the belief of scarcity. Oxfam's study of wealth and inequality reported that – on current trends – by 2016, 1% of the world's population will own more wealth than the other 99%. [43]

So what type of world would we create if we allowed the belief of scarcity to dissolve?

What if the belief was based on abundance?

How would your life change if you held this view?

---

[42] http://www.bbc.co.uk/news/business-15198789/ 10/07/2016/17.50
[43] https://www.theguardian.com/business/2015/jan/19/global-wealth-oxfam-inequality-davos-economic-summit-switzerland/ 10/07/16/18.00

When you live a heart led approach to life and reflect on the things that are of real value, we would change our perception. We would soon realise that what our heart values are those things that we can't put a price on. The things that are of greatest value and enrich us are loving relationships – family, friends, life itself. Is your life guided by this truth or something else?

Several years ago, our dog Jasper was involved in a hit-and-run. Jasper was a very strong character. He was definitely the master of the house, a loving dog but totally independent and un-trainable. We lived opposite a beautiful nature reserve. It was his favourite place, and although he had the opportunity to visit at least twice a day during his scheduled walks, for him this wasn't enough, so on any occasion possible he would dart across the road and walk himself. He had done this on so many occasions, but this time he was unlucky and got hit by a car. He sustained really serious injuries. The diagnosis was grim. The impact of the car had caused damage to his back, broken his two back legs, and fractured his pelvis. Luckily, we were able to get him to the vet within twenty minutes of the incident.

The vet who saw Jasper was amazed with his determination to live. He was surprised that Jasper had not died on impact. Due the severity of his injuries, there was only one specialist hospital in the London that had the level of expertise to operate. It was two hours drive away. The vet wasn't able to give me any guarantees on whether he would survive. We had recently moved back to London from Sweden. I hadn't got around to taking out pet insurance. The vet had told me that the cost of the treatment was going to be in the region of three thousand pounds. This was a lot of money. I spoke to my two children and told them that if I proceeded with treatment, it would mean that we would not be able to go on holiday and we would have to cut back on a few things so that I could pay the vet bills. They agreed immediately, unable to imagine a life without Jasper. I finally reached the hospital after two hours of driving across London. Although Jasper had been sedated, he was whimpering and crying all the way, and so was I. The vet had notified the hospital that I was on my way, and they took Jasper in immediately to assess the full extent of his injuries. After what seemed like a lifetime they called me in and told me the true extent of his injuries. When they showed me the X-rays I was horrified. They said that he had sustained serious damage to his back and they were not sure if he was paralysed. They said that they were happy to operate, but they estimated that the vet bill would be around five thousand pounds. At that point I had to make a decision. Was

I prepared to put him to sleep because I didn't want to pay the vet bills? I didn't have that sort of money to hand over, and I didn't know how I was going to find the money, but I also knew that if there was even the slightest chance of saving Jasper, that was exactly what I was going to do.

Jasper was a member of our family and we loved him dearly. He had given us unconditional love and so much joy, and although the estimated fee was a significant expense, I realised in that moment that I could not put a price on love.

The hospital said that I didn't need to pay the money up front and that I could pay interest free instalments for as long as I needed. I knew in my heart I had made the right decision, the hospital's generosity and flexibility was proof of that. Jasper had several three- to five-hour operations to realign his spine and to pin and plate his legs and pelvis. All the surgeons were impressed with his fight for life. It was clear that Jasper wasn't going to give up, so I figured why should we. He was such a perfect patient in hydro therapy that the staff at the hospital asked if they could feature Jasper in a training film on hydrotherapy treatment for trainee vets. Of course I agreed. Jasper was a star in so many ways. He was such a keen swimmer, and unfortunately he managed to dislodge some of the screws in his back legs whilst swimming, so they had to undertake yet another three-hour operation. The total cost of the vet bill was over eight thousand pounds, and to us it was worth every penny. Jasper had a full recovery, and we had the opportunity to enjoy and additional eight years with him before he passed. This whole experience showed me that love is beyond value. I paid the bill via monthly instalments. What was amazing was that we didn't need to cut back as I had thought. We managed somehow and we still went on holiday. But most importantly we had the pleasure of joy and unconditional love of Jasper in our life. When you are guided by love, everything is possible, and my experience with Jasper was testimony to that.

How to Release Yourself from the Belief of Scarcity

- Each morning when you wake and before you go to sleep, think about the things in your life that you appreciate and are grateful for. Life is meant to be a celebration. So always take time out remind yourself of the wonder of life and the little things that bring you joy. When we do this we immediately lift our sprit and life feels good.

Start this exercise now by noting down the things that you value and appreciate most that cannot be purchased with money.

• Remember that the things that really matter are priceless and abundant. We are blessed with so many things, but if we don't take the time to acknowledge and appreciate them, the beauty and richness of life can just pass us by unnoticed or appreciated.

Life Is about Winners and Losers

This belief is based on the premise that competition is a necessity and without it we cannot perform at our best. We are led to believe that winning at any cost is okay. When we allow this mind set to govern our behaviour, and act without care and consideration of the wider consequences of our actions, we can negatively affect our quality of life and that of others. A win-lose mentality reduces our ability to identify opportunities to collaborate and cooperate, to create more than the sum of the parts. When we are determined to win at the expense of another person, or another living thing, we become destructive, not creative. When you view the world from a systemic perspective, it becomes very clear that it is not possible to increase the value of the whole by taking. We can generate value only by creating and giving.

Our current economic model very rarely takes into account the true cost of being at the top of the list and generating profit. How would the balance sheet look if we factored in the social and environmental costs associated with doing business? The win-lose mind-set also leads to selfish behaviour, greed and corruption. When people feel that it is okay to win at any cost, they contribute to creating division and separation within society, and the results are what we see in the world today. An iniquitous distribution of wealth in society has a negative side, it usually correlates with high crime rates, civil and societal unrest.

People who feel disadvantaged can easily develop low self-esteem. If they view that they are not worthy and have nothing to lose, they act as if they are losers and begin to depend on others.

Conversely, those that view themselves as material winners live in fear of losing what they have attained and become prisoners of their wealth, both mentally and physically. Both groups of people ultimately lose their freedom and the result is that nobody wins.

The drive to win can also lead to a blind focus on producing results and securing the top position. This is prevalent in the world of business today, where short-term results are pursued without considering the wider implications. People neglect their families and loved ones in the hope of getting a promotion or taking home a bigger pay check. When our world is all about winning and not about *being*, we can miss out on the beauty of life. We have made so many technological advances, life should be easier. However, more than ever people are literally working themselves to death.

We have been so many corporate scandals in the last few decades, fuelled by an insatiable desire to be ranked at the top of the list and to achieve a favourable stock value, i.e., to be a winner. Humanity has paid a heavy price for adopting this narrow perspective. Businesses that were once considered solid institutions have disappeared overnight, many others have had to apply for government bailouts. The principles that drive the economic system has led to the destruction of trillions of dollars in value, achieving the very opposite of what corporations have been designed to do, which is to create value not destroy it. Real value can be generated when businesses are ethical in their conduct and take into account the wider implications of their actions and ensure that all stakeholders benefit from their activities. The purpose of many businesses and institutions today is to look good, not to be good, this is what the winner looser construct demands. This unfortunately is at odds with the creation of something which develops and enhances the whole. The belief that there are winners and losers is based on the principle of robbing Peter to pay Paul. This belief actually limits what we achieve collectively. An excessive desire to win usually leads to value reduction somewhere in the system when the primary focus is to obtain the lion share at the expense of someone or something else. We can see how this has played out in 2008 economic crisis. According to *Bloomberg*, $14.5 trillion, or 33 per cent of the value of the world's companies was written off.

When we examine the consequences of the winner and looser paradigm, the results are devastating. This pervading belief takes hope away from those who are less fortunate. The World Health Organization reports that every year, almost one million people die from suicide; this is a "global" mortality rate of 16 per 100,000, or one death every 40 seconds. In the last 45 years, suicide rates have increased by 60 per cent worldwide.[44]

---

[44] World Health Organisation, 2013

Studies also show that in Europe, that for every 1 per cent rise in the unemployment rate, there is a 0.8 per cent rise in the rate of suicides. homeless people are more likely to complete suicide than the general population. [45]

The winner/loser belief also leads us to make ignorant, ill-informed judgments of others. If a person does not possess objects of wealth, look a certain way, come from a certain background, or hold a certain job, they are considered less important. Externalities are used to decide whether a person deserves respect, food, shelter, and compassion. This paradigm is fundamentally flawed. This is one of the main reasons why there is so much hunger and suffering among millions of people all around the world. How can it be just to say that one life is more valuable than another?

Divide and conquer has proven to be an effective strategy. However , we need to ask ourselves how to create harmony, peace, and sustainable equitable value creation within society? The answer is crystal clear: we need to genuinely care and have compassion for all living things. The truth is that we can all winners, but so many people doubt their

---

[45] Enculescu 2012

83

ability. Believing in yourself is essential to finding your leadership.

If you feel that you are missing something in life, then you probably are, but the chances are that you are looking in the wrong place to fill the void. Material objects will never make you feel good about yourself in the long term. You will start to find what you are looking for when you choose to love, appreciate, and forgive yourself.

Leadership is something that we all have inside. If you look deep enough and become still, you will find it. We need to develop a sense of care, not only for our own well-being but also for others. But I have discovered that the before we can have compassion for others, we must first love ourselves.

There is nothing wrong with becoming wealthy; however, the way this wealth is generated is what matters.

The Dalai Lama says that leaders need "ethical discipline". This means that the source of wealth should have been earned honestly, in other words, not at the expense of another person or our ecosystem.

Developing a respect for ourselves is crucial to dissolving the win-loss mentality. Then you will be able to "treat others how you would like to be treated". Each person on this planet is a valuable member of our global community. None of us are perfect, but every person should be treated with respect.

A human being is a part of the whole called by us universe, a part limited in time and space. He experiences himself, his thoughts and feeling as something separated from the rest, a kind of optical delusion of his consciousness. This delusion is a kind of prison for us, restricting us to our personal desires and to affection for a few persons nearest to us. Our task must be to free ourselves from this prison by widening our circle of compassion to embrace all living creatures and the whole of nature in its beauty.

—Albert Einstein

We Are Disconnected and Separate

The Art of Peace is medicine for a sick world. There is evil and disorder in the world because people have forgotten that all things emanate from one source. Return to that source and leave behind all self-centered thoughts, petty desires, and anger. Those who are possessed by nothing possess everything.

—Morihei Ueshiba

This is the greatest belief that deceives us. The truth is we are one. Separation is a creation of the ego and the mind and reinforced throughout society. For eons it has been asserted that we are separate from creative source from which we were created, but how can that be? An artist cannot say that the poem or the painting or the song that they have created is separate and not a part of them. How can you be separate from something that you have created or something that created you?

We live on one planet. If you view earth from space we see one unified whole. All the divisions that exist are divisions we have created. This planet is a place of wonderful diversity. When we combine our differences, we become strong. When we amplify differences, we become weak. The belief of separation is the belief that prevents us from connecting with our soul, because when you feel that something is not part of you, you don't even acknowledge its existence. A fulfilled life is achieved when you choose to live in unity. When we go through life knowing that we are one, life takes on a totally different form. You see every other person and living thing as part of you. You hold everyone and everything with genuine affection, because you know everything is part of you and you are part of everything.

We live in the planetary age, an age of connectedness and interdependence. Our wellbeing and quality of life is dependent on others, and in turn we are dependent on nature to provide us with the air we breathe and the water we drink. Separation is the belief that divides and limits what we can achieve, individually and together.

You exist because of the energetic life force that flows through your body. Physics has proven that energy never disappears – it just changes form. The core of your being is eternal. What we refer to as death as the transition from one form of energy to another. Know that you have always been and will always be part of creation and the creative force. This may be contrary to what you believe, but it is true.

We humans, like every living thing, are part of nature. Why do you think that we are so attracted to the sunrise and sunset? To the oceans rivers and seas? The beauty of a flower. It's because the life energy that brings these things of beauty into being is the same energy that gives us life. We share the same creative life-giving, universal force. This is the creative power of light and love, the source that has brought you and me and the rest of humanity into being. This is what connects us.

No one can become self-actualised without relationship. It is through relationships that we are able understand ourselves and the world around us. When you develop a purposeful relationship with yourself (with your soul), you will discover the relationship that you have with the whole.

When you foster division rather than unity, your efforts will amount to very little. It is said that "no one is an island", and this is true. Separation is an illusion. Happiness, joy and sorrow are universal emotions that we all experience. Human beings have more similarities than differences, yet we tend to focus on our differences which then fuel and reinforce the belief of separation.

The field of quantum physics has discovered that at the subatomic level, we all form part of an "unified energy field". This has been described pure consciousness. We now know that unity is a fundamental law of life and creation. If we hold beliefs that are contrary to this truth, we will lose out on experiencing life in its highest form. It is important as you navigate through life and make choices, that unity exists in all things.

The twin proton experiment which was conducted by Dr. Nicolas Gisin in 1997 demonstrated the mysterious long-range connections that exist between " quantum events" , one particle was split into two and separated but despite this, one of the photons "knew" what happened to its distant twin, and mimicked the twin's response.[46]

The results of this experiment indicate that there is something that connects all things, but it is not visible, or fully understood.

One way we can live fulfilling lives is to live with the intention of enriching the whole. This is the meaning behind "give and so you will receive". Once you discover the joy of life and are guided by the love in your heart, you will be compelled to connect with and share it with others, because this represents the true essence of who you really are.

From the viewpoint of absolute truth, what we feel and experience in our ordinary daily life is all

---

[46] Brown 1997

delusion. Of all the various delusions, the sense of discrimination between oneself and others is the worst form, as it creates nothing but unpleasantness for both sides. If we can realize and meditate on ultimate truth, it will cleanse our impurities of mind and thus eradicate the sense of discrimination. This will help to create true love for one another. The search for ultimate truth is, therefore, vitally important.

—Dalai Lama

Power and Domination Gives Us Freedom

Throughout history, war has been a feature of human civilisation. This is fuelled by the belief that if you overpower another person, this will somehow secure your freedom and liberty.

When you combine the win-loss mentality, the separation belief, and the belief in power and domination, it's easy to see why some people become obsessed position and status. If unchecked, such individuals develop an unjustified sense of superiority and a mistaken sense of importance. The dominated can become increasingly subservient, as their confidence diminishes, or they may become angry and vengeful. In either case, the ability to perform effectively is impacted. People who overpower others create negative emotions like fear, insecurity and anger.

The lack of challenge that those in authority receive, reinforces the belief in their importance and superiority. They feel justified in their behaviour and deserving of their status and position. But have they achieved freedom? The by-product of this belief has created the culture and environment we see today. Those who use their power to defeat others become entangled by the power they wield and the negative view they hold of people. Any person that voices a view contrary to their own is seen as a threat, to be removed if necessary, so they never hear the truth. They also take on too much, as they don't believe that others are capable. This leads to stress and poor decision making. Their lack of trust in others and obsession with power feeds their fear of failure, and over time they become less effective. In an attempt to achieve and dominate, they become more and more authoritarian and very often paranoid. This doesn't sound like freedom to me. In summary, the person who carves out a position of authority through domination is constantly at war with themselves and with others.

Those that allow themselves to be dominated become riddled with fear, they relinquish their voice and become submissive to people have a position or an assigned status, consequently a dysfunctional environment is created and a lack of authenticity prevails. This proves that there is some truth in the saying "power corrupts".

No one can be free if they live in fear. If you recognise yourself as a person who has used your power and position excessively, it's time to forgive yourself and let go of the past so you may transform. Consider how you can give power back to those who have become disempowered through your behaviour. Think about areas in your life where you can support and encourage others to grow and take on more responsibility. Look for the positive attributes of the people around you and show appreciation. If you feel that you have been overpowered, find it in your heart to forgive and start to acknowledge and appreciate who you are.

I believe all suffering is caused by ignorance. People inflict pain on others in the selfish pursuit of their happiness or satisfaction. Yet true happiness comes from a sense of peace and contentment, which in turn must be achieved through the cultivation of altruism, of love and compassion, and elimination of ignorance, selfishness, and greed.

—Dalai Lama

We Are Disempowered and Others Are Responsible

Finding your leadership requires that you take ownership for your life. When we fail to take responsibility, we inadvertently give our energy and power to others. This is what the majority of humanity has done, and we can see the consequences. As mentioned earlier, we all contribute to the collective field of consciousness. Your thoughts and emotions, both positive or negative, feed the field because you are part of the whole.

Accepting the belief that you are disempowered is like throwing in the towel, and you deny yourself access to you true potential. You are an amazing person with unlimited potential. When you affirm and acknowledge that you are responsible for what you experience each and every day and you decide to do something about it, by acting responsibly you can transform your life. Remember, the start of any change is only a thought away.

So where do you need to direct your attention and energy? and What difference can you make?

Exercise Making a Difference

- Become centred in your heart. Take a few deep breaths. The in and out breaths should be of equal length. Repeat this until you fell heart-centred.
- Visualise a picture of the world and take this into your heart.
- Continue to breathe deeply whilst holding the picture of the world in your heart. Feel your heart making a connection to the world, with humanity and every living thing
- Tune into the things that you really care about
- Ask how you can make a difference to the world.
- Wait for the answer to emerge from the silence, stay focused on what you hear and feel.

Record your insights in the space provided or in your journal:

Become aware of how you interact and relate to world. None can take power from you unless you give them the permission. So it's up to you to take charge of your life experience.

The beliefs that I have shared with you are all-pervasive and omnipresent, so much so that we fail to notice them. These paradigms are an integral part of our society, they playout wherever you look, in politics, business, in the media, in education. When we change our beliefs, we will start to change our world.

In 1935, Dr Rupert Sheldrake a Biologist and author discovered *morphic resonance.* He found that when a critical mass of a species acquires certain knowledge, this new level of awareness is fed into the non-local field, and a shift occurs in the universal level of consciousness. The knowledge then becomes common to all members of the species. This phenomenon is very similar to how content on the Internet becomes viral. Research has revealed that the main reason that Internet content goes viral is that it evokes our emotions. When information goes viral, it is circulated to millions of people all around the world in a relatively short period of time. The BBC reported in December 2012, that Gangnam Style has become the first video to clock up more than one billion views on YouTube , it only took 6 months for the views to exceed one billion. The only difference between viral content on the Internet and morphic resonance is that the shift in consciousness and knowing occurs at a frequency we cannot see. It is, however, something that you can feel. Make positive strides to build a relationship with your heart, and align your emotions and actions to the desires of your soul. This is the most important thing you can do for yourself and the world around you.

We must be the change we wish to see.

—Mahatma Gandhi

Change starts with desire. If you have a desire to live a fulfilling life, where you experience joy and happiness, then finding your leadership is for you.

The work starts with you taking responsibility for building a relationship with your heart. The more you open the door to your heart, the stronger the connection will be. It takes practice and perseverance, but every effort that you make will be rewarded.

When we have a desire, we engage with the energy of creation. With heightened awareness, what you desire will become a conscious and deliberate act. Wherever you put your attention, energy flows. You are able to tap into your full potential when you choose to attract and experience the things that serve your best interest and the interest of the whole.

Throughout history many there have been individuals who have found their leadership and in doing so have made a positive contribution to society. When people are inspired and they decide to change something that is what occurs, things change.

When we work with others who share our passion and vision, the process of change can be very powerful. The physical removal of the Berlin Wall was not authorised by the government of the time, they announced that the boarder would be opened for private trips to the West, but it was the people started to dismantle the wall. Throughout history people have joined together and used non-violent means to facilitate positive change. When we act responsibly and join together, we become empowered and find the strength to lead change in ourselves, which in turn has a positive impact in the world.

Today the predominant paradigm of humanity is based on the limitations of our existence – in other words, what we *can't* do. The truth, however, is that we are part of a universal consciousness that has unlimited possibilities. When you start to increase your level of awareness and align your belief system to one that is in sync your original blueprint, you will discover your unlimited source of power.

The change that you are being asked to make is something that you have total control of. In fact, no one else can help you to find your leadership. It's all down to you.

You have the capacity to create whatever you desire and believe. You are doing this as you read this book. The majority of people feel that they cannot make a difference and that they are victims of circumstance, but nothing could be further from the truth.

I believe in the potential that we all have as human beings. All you need to do is travel the journey and stay on the path that will reveal the leader in you.

Are you ready to create a new reality that is founded on a set of beliefs that serve your highest purpose?

Your time is limited, so don't waste it living someone else's life. Don't be trapped by dogma – which is living with the results of other people's thinking. Don't let the noise of others' opinions drown out your own inner voice. And most important, have the courage to follow your heart and intuition.

—Steve Jobs

What If: The Power of Beliefs

We consume and hoard because we believe in scarcity.

We wage war because we believe we are disconnected.

We live in fear because we believe that there is a limit to our existence.

We seek power and domination because we believe this gives us liberty.

We believe nature is there to serve our existence.

The opposite is the truth.

There is abundance.

There is unity in all that exists.

We are eternal.

Freedom is born out of compassion and unconditional love.

We are part of nature.

—Jennifer Rhule

Finding Your Chosen Path

If you haven't found it yet, keep looking. Don't settle. As with all matters of the heart, you'll know when you find it. And, like any great relationship, it just gets better and better as the years roll on.

—Steve Jobs

Have you ever asked yourself why you are here and what life is about. If you haven't, don't you think that it's time that you did?

Just take a minute to acknowledge and appreciate the wonder of life. You started as one cell, and now you consist of billions of cells. Your body is an amazing system of creation capable of performing numerous tasks simultaneously, many of which are performed without you even being conscious or aware. But you are more than a physiological machine. We are not just here to exist within our body.

So what is the purpose for your coming into being? From the moment we enter this world we start the journey of exploration and discovery our desire to learn is programmed into our original blueprint.

Unfortunately, the traditional approach to education is focussed on presenting information and facts and seeking the expected answers rather than encouraging inquiry, curiosity, and self-discovery.

"Inquiry" is defined as "a seeking for truth, information, or knowledge – seeking information by questioning."[47]

Infants begin to make sense of the world by inquiring. From birth, babies observe faces that come near, they grasp objects, they put things in their mouths, and they turn toward voices. The process of inquiring begins with gathering information and data through applying the human all the senses. As we grow older we can often loose the desire to inquire, we become more reserved and less inquisitive, particularly if we feel that we will be judged by the type of questions we ask. Consequently, our view of ourselves and the world around us is formed by the type of information that is presented to us rather than exploration and discovery.

---

[47]Collins English Dictionary 2013

Inquiry takes you from the known to the unknown, and it's in the place of the unknown where unlimited possibilities and truth is waiting to be explored, when we venture into this space, we expand and increase our consciousness.

Finding your leadership can be achieved through inquiry and living a heart-led life. Exploration and learning needs to become an integral part your way of life. What is intriguing to me, is that the more that I learn, the more I realise that we are only scratching the surface of our knowledge and wisdom.

We all have a life force that goes beyond the frame of our body, and this is the part of our self that we need to engage if we are to realise our full potential and become all we can be.

The only thing that interferes with my learning is my education.

—Albert Einstein

As I mentioned at the start of this book, our pursuit of happiness can be an arduous one. Many of us go through life trying to generate feelings of happiness and contentment through activity and acquisition – holidays, buying our dream house or car, acquiring a job title, or accumulating money in the bank. It is time to ask a fundamental question: will these type of activities ever bring us lasting happiness? Both you and I know that material possessions can and do generate feelings of happiness, but the problem is that they do not stay with us for long. In an attempt to repeat the brief experience of happiness, we continue the path of acquisition and accumulation. This approach to living can easily become addictive. I use the term "addition" because it accurately describes the trap in which so many people find themselves.

Here is a definition of addicition:

Addiction is the continued use of a mood altering substance or behavior despite adverse dependency consequences ... Addictions can include, but are not limited to, drug abuse, exercise abuse, sexual activity and gambling. Classic hallmarks of addiction include impaired control over substances or behavior ... Habits and patterns associated with addiction are typically characterized by immediate gratification (short-term reward), coupled with delayed deleterious effects (long-term costs)[48]

The short-term reward in this case is the sensation of achievement. This in itself is not bad. The problem arises when these behaviours are exercised in a culture that reinforces the beliefs of consumption, separation, competition, and power. There is no doubt that the combination of these beliefs create long-term harm to us individually and collectively. When you live a life that is bounded by these illusions, you drift away from your divine right to freedom and joy. Your true self can never be satisfied with the type of happiness that is associated with possessions. That is why the feelings of euphoria is short lived. This path will lead to suffering and misery.

Why does this happen? Because your life energy is being misdirected. The results can be seen everywhere, as people become detached from who they who we truly are and lose their human authenticity. When you start to define yourself by what you have (external attributes) and not by who you truly are, you diminish the very essence of what it means to be human. Your life energy, of

---

[48] Wikipedia2013

which happiness is an intrinsic part of you. We can grow and expand only when we nurture a heartfelt relationship with ourselves and all living things.

True happiness can only be found within yourself. You will probably find this difficult to accept, but it's true. How are you living your life? Is it in the pursuit of external things? How addicted are you to acquiring things that you believe will make you happy?

When you are discontent, you always want more, more, more. Your desire can never be satisfied. But when you practice contentment, you can say to yourself, "Oh yes – I already have everything that I really need."

—Dalai Lama

Are you are living a life that brings you and the world around you freedom, joy, and timeless happiness? If not, it's time to change.

How much of your time and energy, thoughts and emotions, do you direct to the things that really matter? Is your life guided by an inspiring meaningful purpose? Or are you just going through the motions without a destination in mind? We all know that if we start a journey but we don't know where we are going, we are bound to get lost.

The title of this book includes the word "Find". This is deliberate, because most of us go through life looking for something. The ultimate discovery is finding meaning and purpose to our lives. This is part of our original blueprint. I believe that this is what we are hardwired to do, why we are all here. You were born with the wonder of curiosity.

"Why" is a question that is common to all of us. Can you remember asking why as a child? How often do you ask this question now?

The question why is the facilitator for increasing our awareness and level of consciousness. It is often said that in every question there is an answer. Have you ever asked why you are here? It is only when you ask this question – not in your head but in your heart – that you get an answer that reveals the universal truth.

Your life quest is to find the answer to the real purpose of your life. The answers may not come all at once, but the more you ask why, the more will be revealed, and you will be guided on your path to realising your full potential.

Your beliefs define who you are and your emotions create what you experience. when we find the courage to go beyond our fears and ego, a new reality comes into being. This is where the unknown is revealed and your unlimited connection to power and source can be found. Become the observer and you will start to understand the meaning of life.

Life is not about the accumulation of things; in fact, it is the opposite. It is about letting go of the aspects of your life that do not contribute to improving your well-being and the world around you. Just as I had to reduce the weight of my baggage on my vision quest, you too are called to examine your life and let go of those things that limit your experience of life – fear, doubt, anger, envy, separation, competition, and apathy.

- How do you want to be regarded at the end of your life?
- What legacy do you want to leave behind?
- How do you want to be remembered?

Devoting all your effort to superficial things is not just a waste of time. More importantly, it is a waste of your life. This is a truth that you will discover when you find the leader in you.

If you choose to live your life guided by a misdirected purpose, you will find yourself in a place that you don't want to be. By discovering your purpose, you will find true meaning and the inspiration to fufill your dreams .

Suffering is a result of not knowing the true nature of reality. Your ego and current idea of self is not who you truly are.

So ask yourself, if I am not who I think I am, who am I?

Exercise Who Am I ?

Read the statements below and listen to your heart, then complete each statement.

- Become heart centred.
- Connect with your heart, and then shift all the thoughts to your heart. Once you feel centred in your heart, breathe deeply and visualise a golden light radiating from your heart up through your head. Continue to breathe deeply. When you feel connected to your heart, complete each of the statements. Listen to the answer that comes from your

heart and note the first think that comes to you. Be spontaneous.

Ensure that you are heart centred and continue to breathe deeply as you complete each statement. If you find your mind drifting or thinking about other things. Take a few deep breaths, reconnect with your heart, and progress through the exercise.

I Am happiest when ...

I Am joyful when ...

I Am energised when ...

I Am creative when ...

I Am appreciated for ...

I Am enjoying life when ...

I Am generous when ...

I Am recognised for ...

I Am living my dream when ...

I Am productive when ...

I Am generous when ...

I Am at ease when ...

I Am at my best when ...

I Am here to make a positive difference to ...

Review your responses. This will reveal your life's vision, your life purpose's, what is important to you, and your unique skills and abilities.

Now write your vision and life purpose is to (your inspiration):

My vision:

The things value most are: ... ...

I Am is an affirmation of your true self. As I have mentioned numerous times already, whatever you think about yourself, you become, so remember not to put yourself down or attach a negative or derogatory term to *I Am*.

Your response to each of the statements above is a message from your soul.

You may find that what emerged surprised you, but this is the truth of who you are and what your life is about. The demands of everyday life can often take us away from our heart's desire, so it is important that we take time to check in now and again to remind ourselves about what we love doing and what brings us joy, then to create space for yourself to reconnect to your true essence.

When you live a life that is aligned with your values, you reflect your true being. When you live your soul purpose, you become aligned with your authentic self.

Make the decision to live your highest truth. This process may take some time, but it will be worth the effort. It is time to peel back the layers of your identity, the parts you have created that have served you up until now but are no longer required.

So many people devote most of their lives being someone else, without even being conscious of the fact. Some find themselves trying to be what their parents what them to be, others lose themselves as they attempt to fit in with their peers, while others allow themselves to be defined by their work environment or material wealth. You are not your job, position, car, house, or the size of your bank account. You are far greater than all of that. If we choose to live a life that is not aligned with our soul purpose, we will create dis-ease within us. Our physical body is a useful barometer for letting us know if we are on the right track. You will know when you are living a life that is aligned to you purpose and vision because you will have the vitality to achieve your ambitions and goals, whilst experiencing an inner sense of calm and peace. When we drift into living a life that is focussed on the things that are outside of us, we can become increasingly detached from our true nature.

When you live in accordance with your soul purpose with love, your life will be in "flow". This means that you are attuned to your natural strengths and abilities and are guided by your higher self.

In our global interconnected world there are many opportunities to show up and lead, not from a position of power but from a place of knowing with love. When you move through life with this orientation, every positive feeling, thought, and act radiates into the non-local field, of which you are an integral part. When you raise your vibration and frequency, you contribute to raise the frequency and vibration of the whole. This is why you are so important. Your thoughts and emotions feed the universal field of consciousness.

The vision and purpose that you have crafted is part of your original blueprint. Now that you have, remembered it, you can move forward with renewed clarity and intent.

Now is the time to step forward and start the journey that leads to the realisation of yourself. Have faith in and know that within, you have the source of unlimited potential.

From a Grain of Sand

You were there at the beginning of time.

Your energy has existed from the beginning of time, just like a grain of sand.

Wrapped in total love and light, find your way home.

—Jennifer Rhule

The purpose of our life needs to be positive. We weren't born with the purpose of causing trouble, harming others. For our life to be of value, I think we must develop basic good human qualities- warmth, kindness, compassion. Then our life becomes more meaningful and more peaceful – happier.

—Dali Lama

Bringing Good Things to Life

The Light

You were there at the beginning of time

A place where everything and nothing exists.

The sea of consciousness and unlimited possibilities.

The light of love ignites you.

You are united with your source what is and has always been.

Wrapped in total love and light, you are home from where you came.

—Jennifer Rhule

I was inspired to write the above after completing a meditation course in June 2002. The core of this message came to me again during my second sweat lodge in Mexico, in December 2012. The heat of the sweat lodge was just as intense as it had been my first time ten years earlier, but my experience was different. Lacking fear, I was now able to embrace the experience, and the limitations of my ego soon dissolved. I was privileged to experience what I can only describe as the totality of my being, a place of unity, harmony, love, and peace. When we were asked at the end of the sweat to share what had occurred, my response was, "Everything and nothing at the same time." On one level this was a strange thing to say, but on another I knew that I had experienced a deep truth. I have been writing a journal for many years. In the process of writing this book, I read through this journal, and I found this poem.

This poem encapsulates the meaning of life, which it is to live our lives consciously, gaining access to all of our potential. The leader within is not about exerting power and control over another person. It concerns achieving mastery of yourself – your thoughts, feelings, and emotions – and living a life with meaning and purpose.

Think about some of the people that are considered great leaders of our time – Nelson Mandela, Mother Teresa, Martin Luther King jr, Mahatma Gandhi. I'm sure that you have many other examples. These wonderful human beings started out just like you and me. They achieved great things because they were inspired by a vision greater than themselves. Their deep love for humanity gave them the courage and conviction to bring good things to life.

All these individuals carved out a new and better path for humanity. All of had the courage to speak their truth, they were free from fear, and spoke openly from their heart.

Our lives begin to end the day we become silent about things that matter.

—Martin Luther King Jr

These individuals were not bounded by the beliefs and conventions of the time. They articulated a vision that resonated with the heart's desires of many, and in doing so they helped others to also find their leadership.

An individual has not started living until he can rise above the narrow confines of his individualistic concerns to the broader concerns of all humanity.

—Martin Luther King Jr

Inspired by a vision they lived a purposeful life. They did not waver when they met resistance. They found the strength to overcome the setbacks and obstacles that attempted to hinder their path. They demonstrated power of humility, forgiveness, and living in the present. They were able to let go of pain and hurt so that they were free in the moment to make intelligent choices.

The weak can never forgive. Forgiveness is the attribute of the strong.

—Mahatma Gandhi

These individuals were not assigned a position of authority. They were granted authority as a consequence of their conduct. They were respected for their courage, wisdom, and their compassion. They had a generosity of heart, and they devoted their lives to be in the service of others.

You, like me, have these human qualities. They are innate part of us. When you chose to live a heart-led life they naturally become part of your character.

People who find their leadership choose to live in harmony with their soul's purpose and in doing so realise their full potential, and so can you. All you need to do is raise your consciousness. You will know you have achieved your leadership ascent when you ;

- Actively pursue your soul's vision and purpose
- Let go of fear and embrace the power of unconditional love
- Live an authentic, heart-led life
- Trust your intuition and inner wisdom
- Forgive others and live in the present moment
- Become the observer and transcend the limitations of your ego
- Have good intent and live in a way that brings good things to life
- Have care and compassion for all living things
- Respect and love yourself
- Treat others the way you would like to be treated
- Act in the knowledge that there is unity in all things
- Live knowing that your thoughts and emotions are acts of creation
- Live knowing that your level of consciousness contributes to the consciousness of the whole
- Focus your energy on the things you love and care about

The Power of Love

The power of love brings light where there is darkness.

The power of love brings hope when there is fear.

The power of love creates unity when there is separation and abundance when we feel poor.

The power of love gives us energy when we are tired.

Invite the unlimited power of love.

—Jennifer Rhule

Becoming the Conductor

Be clear about your intentions. You put your thoughts into motion by adding energy to them (your emotion). Know that you possess the gift of creation

As a conductor of your life, you need to consciously direct your activities and emotions so that they are aligned with your vision, purpose, and values. Becoming aware of how you react to situations and developing the ability to take a pause will help you to disconnect from any negative habitual emotional reactions that are not in your best interest of you or others. The amygdala is located in the centre of the brain, stores memories of different experiences and our emotional reactions to them. It is often referred to as the primitive part of our brain. It causes us to react instinctively to situations based on prior experience, particularly those that we perceived as threatening. When you take a pause and become heart centred. You can then make a conscious choice about how to act, rather than just reacting. Becoming heart-centred, taking a deep breath, and becoming the observer for just a fraction of a second is all you need to engage with all of your intelligence. When you connect with your heart and actively engage the part of your brain that aids conscious thought, you tap into your infinite wisdom. A pause enables you to disconnect from your instinctive response and gain access to a higher state of consciousness and intelligence. When we are fearful or feel insecure, our unconscious reaction is to defend our position.

Your ability to lead for good will develop when you take the time to check in with your heart, particularly in situations when you feel vulnerable, angry, or threatened. Acknowledging how you feel, and making a conscious-hearted choice can transform the moment. The truth is that many of the things we fear are creations of the mind. They are not real; we just think they are. The present moment provides each of us with the opportunity to find our leadership; however, this will occur only if we remain conscious and alert, unbounded by past experience or fear of the future Remember, only you can decide what you feel. Very often we blame others for what we experience, but the truth is that we are totally responsible, you are the creator. We all have the freedom of choice to decide how to react to each situation.

Whenever you feel a negative emotion (angry, upset, frustrated), remember that you are the one that engendered that feeling. Negative emotions create an imbalance within us. We all know that we are not very intelligent when we are upset, so the smart thing to do when we feel this way is to take a few deep breaths and become heart-centred. It takes only a few seconds to gain a sense of equilibrium in the present moment. Whenever your thoughts are charged with a negative feeling, develop the habit of asking yourself two important questions:

- What is my motivation (fear or love)?
- Who will benefit (myself or others)?

Each moment in life is precious. When we hold the intention to show up at our best and choose to be guided by love and service to others, we increase our ability to experience joy and happiness.

Becoming GREAT

Every day, people settle for less than they deserve.
Every human being has the potential for greatness.

—Bo Bennett

The creation of something good cannot be taken for granted. It takes time, dedication, and perseverance. Your journey starts with just one choice. When you decide that you want to transform and experience the best that life has to offer, the journey begins. It is important to remember that you bring things into existence through the choices that you make. Never underestimate your true power.

I have said this before and I will say it again. You have a very important role to play in the evolution of humanity. You are being called to find your leadership, because this is your inheritance, and you have the potential to be GREAT. You have unlimited power, wisdom, and talents. All of this will come into being when you are confident in your ability. Choose to live a heart-led life and be inspired to make a positive contribution.

With realization of one's own potential and self-confidence in one's ability, one can build a better world.

—Dalai Lama

At this stage of your journey you would have discovered your life's vision and purpose. You can bring this into being when your life is inspired by the power of love. Love is the original creative force of life. We all, regardless of how we chose to live our life, carry the light of love within us. Through our choices we can allow our light to radiate or diminish.

Spread love everywhere you go. Let no one ever come to you without leaving happier.

—Mother Teresa

Becoming GREAT will enable you to play a conscious active role in creating a better world for yourself and in doing so contribute to the transformation of the whole.

Finding your leadership requires that raise your level of consciousness, that you ascend your being.

This is something you need to nurture and invest in each day. The more time you devote to the practice becoming GREAT, the more it will become a way of life. It is just like training for the marathon, firstly you need to be inspired to reach your goal, which in this case is to realise your full potential as a human being. Through practice and repetition and developing your ability to manage your thoughts and emotions, your experience of the world will change, and being GREAT will become a natural part of you. As humans we have a tremendous capacity to learn and develop. We really don't know we are capable of until we try. Many of us choose to believe that we are limits to what we can achieve, individually and collectively, and that we can't change the way things are. It's just the way life is. However, you can decide to take another point of view. If you consider that what we experience in our life and the world today been created by us. If we don't like what we see, we can change it. Your role is to contribute to the creation of a new story. There is no reason why we should continue on the current road, particularly when we can see where the road is heading.

Nothing changes if we continue to think, feel, and act the way we have always done. We all need to wake up the truth about life. This is what this book is about. Your true power and wisdom can never found outside you. The more you are able to let go of your fears, your need for security, or any other attachment, the happier you will be, and in doing so you are able to transform yourself and the world around you.

You should not underestimate the power of the beliefs you currently hold. I hope that you have started to examine how these inform and shape your perceptions and the way you view the world and live your life. You will find your leadership when you take steps to let go of whatever prevents you from feeling free. These can be thoughts, ideas, beliefs, or even the status you believe you have attained through your work. The truth is these things will never be able to define who you truly are, and the more attention and energy you direct to these things, the more detached you will become from your true essence. Have you ever wondered why people who have attained great wealth and power never seem content, and continue to pursue much of the same? When you decide to act in the way you have always done, you will achieve the same result. There is nothing wrong with enjoying nice things in life. The problem occurs when material things begin to define who you are. When the desire to acquire or retain material things harms another person, creates fear and insecurity, or diminishes the quality of life on our planet, this is a sure sign that you have lost your way.

The current paradigm of scarcity, winners and losers, separation, domination, and disempowerment is all-pervasive. You will need to engage your highest level of intelligence to disengage from these beliefs and to stay on track. Building a strong relationship with your heart and reminding yourself of your soul purpose needs become a regular practice.

Fame or integrity: which is more important? Money or happiness: which is more valuable? Success or failure: which is more destructive? If you look to others for fulfilment, you will never truly be fulfilled. If your happiness depends on money, you will never be happy with yourself. Be content with what you have; rejoice in the way things are. When you realize there is nothing lacking, the whole world belongs to you.

—Lao-tzu

Your personal vision is part of the new story, so become fearless in pursuing it.

Ask yourself, "Who am I?" as often as you can, and your true self will be revealed to you.

A GREAT life contains Generosity, Relationships, Expansion, Appreciation, and Trust. In this section, each of these attributes will be explained in more detail and be accompanied by some practical tools , actions and steps to help you to lead your transformation.

Before reading this section you should have developed a clear understanding of your personal vision and values. If this is still not clear, repeat the Vision, values and purpose exercise.

Re write your vision, purpose, and values below.

My vision is:

My life purpose is:

The things that are most important to me, (my values) :

Your Journey Towards Greatness

Now is the time to embark on becoming GREAT. As you follow this path, you will access your original blueprint, the part of you that has always existed. Finding your leadership is about taking small but significant steps. To start your journey, all you need is a change of mind guided by your heart.

G –Generosity

R –Relationships

E – Expansion

A – Appreciation

T – Trust

Generosity

Kindness in words creates confidence. Kindness in thinking creates profoundness. Kindness in giving creates love.

—Lao Tzu

The smallest act of kindness is worth more than the greatest intention.

—Kahlil Gibran

Generosity, in essence, is all about kindness. Firstly, you need to be kind and compassionate to yourself. When you hold kindness in your heart, you will have the capacity to be kind and compassionate to others. Kindness is about caring enough to do the right thing, in the right way. Kindness brings love into motion. Good things come to life when you care about yourself and the wellbeing of others.

Make philanthropy your currency. Giving is a natural part of us. This is why we feel good when we are able to give of ourselves and be of service. It is a way of letting us know that we have a purpose and intrinsic value within ourselves. The response to the Boxing Day tsunami in 2004 was a wonderful demonstration of the generosity that exists within our global community. About US$14 billion was raised internationally. The generosity that was displayed was unprecedented. In the UK, the government pledged to match the donation made by the public. This generosity inspired others to give, making it one of the most successful fundraising activities of our time.

The more you give of yourself and serve others, the more you will receive and the more happiness you will experience. When you have generosity of heart to give of yourself, you will find abundance and freedom. There is a magical power in giving, so be generous, to yourself and others, without expectation.

Spread love everywhere you go. Let no one ever come to you without leaving happier.

—Mother Teresa

Action Steps: Generosity

Each day, connect with your heart and send love to yourself and all living things. Small acts of kindness can change the world, so develop a *kindness action plan* for a week and then congratulate yourself for what you have managed to achieve. Here are some suggestions:

- Say hello to people you pass on the street.
- Call a friend that you haven't spoken to for a while.
- Invest some time in getting to know a colleague or neighbour.
- Let someone know how much you care about them.
- Offer to help a person who needs some assistance.
- Smile.
- Open the door for a stranger.
- Say thank you to a people that have given you a service e.g., a supermarket assistant.
- Send love to a person that has hurt you.

After you have implemented your plan , take a step back and examine what has changed in , specifically how you view your life. Record the progress that you have made in your journal.

Relationships

Let us always meet each other with smile, for the smile is the beginning of love.

—Mother Teresa

Relationships define who we are and what we become.

The relationships that we have with ourselves defines the type of relationship we create with others and the world. The first and most important relationship is the one that we have with ourselves. You will never find it in your heart to love others if you do not love yourself. The truth is that we can never give another something that we do not possess, so building a loving relationship with yourself is a precondition for loving and caring for others. Having an authentic relationship with yourself is necessary in order to build a positive relationship with the world around you.

Forgiveness is the emotion that allows you to let go of the past so that you are able to give all of your attention to the present. If you choose to carry memories of the past into relationships in the present, you block the opportunity a relationship to grow and for something new and better to emerge. Strengthen your relationship with your heart and develop the ability to listen deeply to the guidance of your soul. Know that you are wise when you engage with all your intelligence, and in doing so, you will grow in confidence and ability.

Meaningful relationships are created when we are honest and genuine with ourselves. Every person we meet provides us with the opportunity to demonstrate our love, care and respect. Be authentic and true in your relationship with others and find the courage speak your truth with compassion.

A lack of transparency results in distrust and a deep sense of insecurity.

—Dalai Lama

Whenever you are in dialogue with others, particularly when trying to find solutions to

problems, hold the intent that you will find a
solution that is mutually beneficial.

You will only be able to create harmony with
others when you have harmony within yourself.
Remember that finding peace can only be found if
this is what you are seeking. Where there is
conflict, be flexible and willing to change your
mind, allow new possibilities to emerge. Welcome
different points of view and be willing to let go of
pre-conceived ideas. Open yourself to your
creativity and the creativity of others. Holding good
intent is all you need to create good relationships.
When you desire to achieve a win-win , the right
solutions will come to light.

Know that you have the power to influence the life
of another. You will know that you have found
your leadership when the intent of your
interactions is to build confidence and inspire
others to give of their best.

Relationship is also about holding others in high
regard. Research has shown that the expectations
you have of another person will influence what that
person can achieve. When you have positive
expectations of another person or situation, this is
what is manifested and experienced; it has also
been proven that the opposite is also true.

Action Steps: Relationships

- Reflect on your beliefs and examine how they influence the nature of your relationship with yourself, with others, and with the world. Identify the shifts in perceptions that are required to create relationships that are based on respect, love, and compassion. Create an action plan detailing how you can increase the respect, love, and compassion that you give to yourself and others. Review your progress on a weekly basis and update your plan where necessary.
- Build confidence in others by giving them your attention, your support and affirming their strengths and unique abilities. Give praise and recognition.
- Invest time in building relationships with people who are different from you. Listen with empathy and care. Be open to the possibility of learning something new. Note in your journal the insights that you have gained through adopting this approach.
- Encourage others to give of their best by holding high expectations of what they can achieve.
- Write a list of people that have hurt you in the past and find in your heart to forgive them.

- Before participating in conversations with people, visualise a win-win outcome that produces mutual benefit.
- Develop opportunities to collaborate and work with others on things that really matter and that you care about.
- Find ways to connect with and support your local community. Become a volunteer.
- Share your skills and experience, become a coach or mentor.

Expansion

If you always put limit on everything you do, physical or anything else. It will spread into your work and into your life. There are no limits. There are only plateaus, and you must not stay there, you must go beyond them ... Ever since I was a child I have had this instinctive urge for expansion and growth. To me, the function and duty of a quality human being is the sincere and honest development of one's potential.

—Bruce Lee

Living your soul purpose with responsibility is about developing an interconnected view of who you are and living in a way that acknowledges that you are an important part of the whole. The more that you expand your view, the more you will come to realise that everything is connected. When you choose to live in unity with all that exists, you let go of the idea of separation or individualism.

For expansion to occur you will need to dissolve any beliefs which hold you back. When this occurs you will gain access to your higher self and the unlimited wisdom and power that is an integral part of you. From a place of stillness and calm you will discover your inner strength. Again this is a gradual process. By devoting parts of your day to being still, you will increase and expand and discover your true identity.

When we choose to be good, we tap into our greatness that already exists within. When you hold love in your heart you will tap into the universal and divine source that exists within all things. When we expand, we treat each moment of our life as an opportunity for growth and potential. This is can be more difficult than it sounds. Just take a moment to think about how you approach your life. Very often, we unconsciously bring past experiences, deeply held views, and negative emotions into the present moment and allow these perceptions to shape the moment and subsequent future. Through reflection and contemplation, you are able to increase your awareness of how you react to situations and take steps to manage your emotions in a positive way, so that you become free from habits, emotions, and beliefs that stifle your growth and evolution.

There is richness in diversity, so embrace it with all your heart. This will lead to increased insight and the true nature of our interdependency. Collaboration and cooperation is the only way we can create a better world for ourselves and humanity. When we choose to work with others in a constructive manner, we combine and multiply our abilities. Dreams can become reality and positive change can be achieved when people join together with a shared vision and purpose. There has never been a greater need than today. Institutions that do not serve the best interest of humanity are being exposed. Through a unified approach and the creation of a new set of beliefs that liberate us, it is possible to create a new way of living.

When people are synchronised in their intent, performance can soar. Misaligned actions divert attention and energy and diminish what can be achieved. Within a framework of collaboration, you can positively contribute to the evolution of humanity.

Become an active member of your global community and remember that you are part of a wonderful whole, where each person has an important role to play. When you acknowledge and use this truth to guide your thoughts and actions, you will be playing your part in creating joy and happiness.

Life finds its purpose and fulfilment in the expansion of happiness.

—Maharishi Mahesh

Action Steps: Expansion

• Devote at least twenty minutes a day to building a relationship with your heart through heart-centred meditation, be still, become heart focused and breathe from the centre of your heart. Note in your journal the insights you gain, act on what comes to light.
• Plan to spend some time each day in nature observe the world around whilst being centred in your heart, note your insights in your journal,

and decide on how they can support your development and growth.

• At the end of each day, reflect on your experiences. Take time out to review your behaviour, your decisions, your social interactions, your feelings, and your emotions. The purpose of these reviews is to identify how performance can be improved, not beat yourself up or blame others. The more that you observe what is going on around you, the more you will see and you will increase your ability to be the conductor of your life.

• Set yourself a goal to create or try something new every day, it doesn't need to be a something major, it just needs to be something different e.g take a different route to work, start a new hobby

• Revisit your vision and values on a monthly basis to help you keep on track. Share your vision with others, and ask for their support and encouragement.

• Before participating in a meeting or a challenging situation, take a few minutes to become heart centred, visualise the meeting going well, imagine a ray of light and love connecting you and all the other people involved. Approach the situation with a positive frame of mind.

• Affirm your greatness and what you have achieved. Become heart centred. Be still and call into being your *I am* presence and visualise and feel the emotion that comes to you and any insights in you journal and act on them wholeheartedly.

- o   I am loving
- o   I am connected to the whole
- o   I am wisdom
- o   I am eternal
- o   I am happy

Appreciation

Be ever-grateful for the gifts received from the universe, your family, Mother Nature, and your fellow human beings.

—Morihei Ueshiba

Find it in your heart to acknowledge and be thankful for what you have in your life, as opposed to what you don't. The more that you focus on the things that are positive in your life, the more positive your life will be come. In addition, it's good for your health. Research studies in the field of psychoneuroimmunology (PNI) have found that subjects who practiced acts of happiness and gratitude had raised energy levels, improved physical health, and less fatigue and pain.

Appreciation is also a way of changing your perception, leading to increased mental clarity and heightened intuitive awareness it helps us put things into perspective and see things differently, this will enable you to engage a higher level consciousness. When this is activated we are able to find intelligent solutions to complex problems. When you believe you can find a solution to a problem, you will. Every experience in life presents itself to you to help you discover something about life, so be grateful for life's challenges.

Ask yourself

- What can I learn from this experience?

Appreciation and gratitude are powerful emotions they can help you gain peace of mind.

Action Steps: Appreciation

- Before going to sleep, give thanks to the positive things you have experienced during your day, the things that made your heart smile.
- When you are feeling down, write a list of all the good things in your life and the things that really matter.

- Whatever life throws at you, remember that they do not define who you truly are. Appreciate the experience and let it go.
- Appreciate the people that are important in your life by spending time with them, maintaining regular contact, and them know why you appreciate them being in your life.

Make it a habit to tell people thank you, to express your appreciation, sincerely and without the expectation of anything in return. Truly appreciate those around you, and you'll soon find many others around you. Truly appreciate life, and you'll find that you have more of it.

—Ralph Marston

Every day, think as you wake up, today I am fortunate to be alive, I have a precious human life, I am not going to waste it. I am going to use all my energies to develop myself, to expand my heart out to others; to achieve enlightenment for the benefit of all beings. I am going to have kind thoughts towards others, I am not going to get angry or think badly about others. I am going to benefit others as much as I can.

—Dalai Lama

Trust

He who does not trust enough, will not be trusted.

—Lao Tzu

To trust others, you must be able to trust yourself. If you find it difficult to trust others, this is a clear sign that you lack confidence in your own discernment and decision making. If you are attached to certainty and control, you will most certainly find it difficult to trust, because trust necessitates a willingness to venture into the unknown. When we choose to trust, the only thing that we can aid us in our decision is hope.

There are essential elements to trust, *reliance, position of obligation,* and *care.* Reliance requires confidence in the presence of your good qualities, especially fairness, truth, honour, and ability. Position of obligation refers to the expectation others have of you to act responsibly or honourably. Care is just as it sounds – the ability to take good care of somebody or something.

Trust is easy to give when you have confidence in your own ability, judgment, and wisdom. Many people believe that trust is about the capability of

153

another person, but the truth is that trust is all about of us. There is a close link between your level of consciousness and your ability to trust. You need to use all the intelligence of your mind, body, and soul to trust. When you embrace the beauty of who you are and engage life wholeheartedly, you will discover that trust is the key to your liberty and freedom. Trust is something that we must give before we can experience it. You may struggle with trust because you want certainty of the outcome, but the reality is you need two things to trust – hope that things will work out the way you intended and forgiveness if they don't.

In life disappointments are guaranteed. After all, we will all make mistakes. When we allow ourselves to be limited by such experiences, we rob ourselves of the opportunity to make the most of the present. Living in the past will guarantee that the past will be repeated. If things don't work out the way we had hoped, see it as an opportunity to develop and grow. Never allow an unpleasant experience to close your heart to trust. The only way you can build trust by giving trust. It is one of the keys to unlocking your human potential and the potential of others, and it is one of the fundamental building blocks of all meaningful relationships. When you are guided by your higher self and the power of love, you are able to use your intuition and gut feeling to discern what is trustworthy. The more conscious you become, the easier it will be to trust. Think about the times in your life when you have been encouraged and trusted by another person. I'm sure you honoured the gift of trust. When we trust, we help people to grow in confidence and capability. If you want someone to take responsibility, you need to be trusting. Most people take ownership when they feel trusted and respected.

Actively encourage open and honest discussion and debate. When you have achieved this, you will know that you have created a climate of trust and respect.

Trust is an inherent part of us. Can you imagine a world where there trust did not exist. It would be a very different place. This is why online trading works. If this was not the case, no one would ever buy something via the Internet. The monetary system was founded on trust, an indication that trust is part our general nature.

Trust is at the core of our being. This is why when it is betrayed, our ability to trust is affected. The good news is that we are living in a world where there is ever-increasing transparency. Systems that are not founded on truth and fairness are being exposed. This helps us to make informed choices

about who and what we can trust. But first and
foremost, trust starts with each of us trusting
ourselves.

*Again, you can't connect the dots looking forward;
you can only connect them looking backwards. So
you have to trust that the dots will somehow connect
in your future. You have to trust in something - your
gut, destiny, life, karma, whatever. This approach
has never let me down, and it has made all the
difference in my life.*

—Steve Jobs

Action Steps: Trust

- Review the areas of your life where you lack
confidence and trust. Identify three key areas
and examine the emotions that are associated
with each situation. Become heart centred and
write against each item on your list a successful
outcome. Develop an action plan listing the
changes that you are committed to make to
ensure, if presented with the same situation
again, you would feel confident and be more
trusting of yourself and others.

- Identify where you can increase the level of trust with your work colleagues, family members, and friends by being more open and authentic. Note the changes you are required to make and develop an implementation plan. Review your accomplishments and the results in your journal.

- Pursue a course of action that supports your personal vision and life purpose, complete tasks and activities that take you out of your comfort zone, embark on achieving your goal wholeheartedly with confidence and trust, review your progress and celebrate your achievements.

Ascension and Your Role

The purpose of your life journey is to discover the GREAT magnitude of who we are.

I truly believe that individuals can make a difference in society. Since periods of change such as the present one come so rarely in human history, it is up to each of us to make the best use of our time to help create a happier world.

—Dali Lama

If the way you are living your life today do does not bring you total happiness and joy, it's time to change. Now is the time to take the necessary steps that will enable you to experience sustainable joy and happiness irrespective of what is going on in the world around you. You have all that you need, however your ascension will take dedication and mastery of what you choose to experience. Our world is evolving, and you, like everyone else, have a responsibility to evolve with it. The way to realise your potential is to become heart led and to direct your energy towards bringing good things in to your life and the lives of others. The things that really matter are priceless, and there is an unlimited and abundant supply of love available to you. In the world today, it is so easy to become estranged from your heart and your soul, so stay connected with your heart and your conscious and ascended self.

Your role is to work in harmony with your soul purpose, the desires of your heart. This is the place where you will discover what really matters. As you pursue your path to freedom and goodness, be inspired by your vision and heart-led purpose.

When each of us employs the best of our human qualities, we make our world and the world around us a better place. So develop the courage to be guided by your heart and soul.

Remember, you are a powerful being. Through your actions, know you are able to raise the consciousness of others, and in doing so lead the transformation to a new way.

There is no limit to what you can achieve when you are inspired by love for yourself, humanity, and all living things. A unified, connected approach to society, business, and humanity is required if we are to create a sustainable future.

We will only progress as a civilisation when we accept that we inhabit the planet as one race and that we are interdependent. Accept diversity for what it is there for: to enrich our life's experience, not to separate and divide us.

Finding your leadership is critical to ensuring we create a future that we want to be part of, one that will support future.

Make the Most of the Gift of the Present

Direct and focus positive thoughts and loving energy emotions to the things that really matter. These should now be clear. If not, repeat the *I am* exercise until you have gained a heart-focussed response to each statement, armed with the clarity of your life's purpose, you are ready to carve out a new path that is in line with the deepest desires of your soul. When you do, you will be free from regret, anger, envy, and fear. We all create these sentiments from time to time, but as the observer you will see that you have the power to change your experience. Your mission is to be the master of what you bring into being.

Realise deeply that the present moment is all you have. Make the *now* the primary focus of your life.

As soon as you honour the present moment, all unhappiness and struggle dissolve, and life begins to flow with joy and ease. When you act out the present-moment awareness, whatever you do becomes imbued with a sense of quality, care, and love—even the most simple action.

—Eckhart Tolle

Heart-led living, in the present moment, is the gateway to your leadership and power. The past has gone, the future will be determined through the way you handle the present.

Be in Love

Throughout this book I have often referred to the power of love and its importance. You've probably worked out by now I am not referring to the sentimental love, associated with attachment, desire, or accumulation. All references to love in this book is referring to love as the creative energy source, the spark that brings newness and wisdom into being. It's time for you to expand into *love*. Love is the energy that unites us all. If you don't believe me, check in with your heart.

With love you will find the passion and courage to find your voice and release yourself from beliefs that limit you can achieve. You will be free when you let go of everything that prevents you from optimising what you can achieve in the present

Be Wise

Wisdom is love and love is wisdom. The wise are those which have discovered the meaning of life and the unlimited potential they possess. They use all their power and intelligence, their mind , body and soul to serve and affect positive change that leads to improving the quality of life for all, not just the selected few. When we act wisely we engage our original blue print and true nature.

Be a Great Human Being

Being human is about expressing the very essence of who we are, which I believe is to be in loving and caring. When we are guided by love and compassion, the connection and relationship that we have with the rest of humanity becomes a natural state. With this perspective, we are able to make decisions that take into account the context of which we are part behave in a way that honours and respects the universal connections that exist.

Expand Your Awareness

We live in a connected world. Our challenge is to live in a way that acknowledges this truth. We also live in a time when the truth is being revealed in so many ways that all you need to do is join up the dots and the full picture will start to reveal itself.

As you increase your level of awareness, you will discover what is in your heart, what you are called to do, and how your talents and abilities can be used to create a positive difference.

Stay connected to all that is, be mindful of the wider implications of your actions, and remember your role is to contribute and enrich the whole

Be Great in Your Work

Your work is going to fill a large part of your life, and the only way to be truly satisfied is to do what you believe is great work. And the only way to do great work is to love what you do. If you haven't found it yet, keep looking. Don't settle. As with all matters of the heart, you'll know when you find it

—Steve jobs

Your primary employment is to serve the desires of your soul. When you follow this path, you will become free of pursue a role in society and a job that brings joy and happiness to your world.

In whatever you are employed, make your place of work a GREAT place where Generosity, Relationships, Expansion, Appreciation, and Trust become integral to the culture and the products and services that you have been engaged to provide. For business to flourish in the twenty-first century and beyond, the primary purpose of the enterprise needs to be wholesome. By this I mean it must extend beyond the sole purpose of achieving profit, at the expense of the quality of life and environment. Business needs your leadership. Play your part in the transformation of business conduct. Your responsibility is to bring life, love, and vitality to everything that we are able to influence. This evolved approach to living helps all of us to perform to the best of our abilities.

The world and life are far too complex and fast moving for any one person or group to take the reins. To create a better world, we all need to play our part. Step forward into the joy of life and make conscious choices about how you direct your energy. Be selective with the types of businesses that you support, and give only to those that practice integrity, fairness, respect, truth, and genuine concern for the environment. You have the power in your hands, through the choices you make, to influence the whole. Wherever possible, support your local community and local businesses. In this way we can start to gain some sense of equilibrium in the world of commerce. Direct our energy, consciously and become an active player in the game of life. You have a responsibly to act responsibility in everything you think and do.

In this fast-paced, complex, and ever-changing environment, we need to develop new approaches to living. Evolving and developing new approaches are essential to ensuring we create a sustainable and joyful future.

We all need to develop tools and techniques that enable us to give our best in all situations. Our intent must be to manifest positive emotions. They energise us, enabling us to use all our cognitive, physiological, and emotional intelligence. In reality, the only thing that we have the capacity control is ourselves. This is where all our attention should be directed. When you create a union between your heart and your mind, you bring harmony into your being and you will become wise beyond measure.

In the introduction of this book I presented some of the challenges that we face, you may not be personally impacted by these events today, but I can assure you that you will in the future. The reason why our current situation prevails is because we allow it to be that way. You can contribute to creating another way. Finding your leadership is the next stage of your and our evolution. It's about creating a space for you to reconnect to the best you can be, your greatness.

If you choose to stand aside and allow the existing paradigm to prevail, you are contributing to maintaining to the status quo. It is time for you and every person you know to find their leadership. Encourage others to free themselves from feelings and beliefs that limit us from being GREAT.

Start off by taking small steps. Little things make a big difference when they are guided by good intent. It is like throwing a pebble into a still lake – there is always a ripple effect. Try it and you will see. The exercises in this book can be repeated numerous times, each practice will lead to discover more of yourself and your leadership.

I welcome you to the community of GREAT individuals who have found their leadership and live a heart-led life. You are now part of an important group of people who will play their part in creating a new way of living, one that brings happiness and joy to the world and leads the transformation of this world to one that is guided by love and compassion for all living things, including our precious planet.

About the Book

We all aspire to attain happiness, peace, and freedom. In this fast-paced, changing, and increasingly demanding world, you can find yourself in a place you don't want to be, having drifted away from the things that really matter.

Find the Leader in You invites you to take an unconventional journey to discover what it takes to achieve success in life with our love ones, in our career, and in the world whilst enjoying every moment.

This guide will help you become the master of your life and realise your full potential as a human being.

Bibliography

- Fox Stuart, (2010). *What Causes Corporate Greed* . Available: www.live Science.com/6394-corporate-greed.html . Last accessed 24th June 2013.

- Jha Alok ,(2005). *Where belief is born.* Available: http://www.guardian.co.uk/science/2005/jun/30/p sychology.neuroscience. Last accessed 24th May 2013.

- McCraty Rollin, Atkinson Mike and Tomasino Dana . (2001). Exploring the Role of the Heart in Human Performance. In: HeartMath Research Center *The Science Of The Heart*. CA: Institute of HeartMath, Publication . No. 01-001 p 4.

- Nelson Roger . (2009). *Meaningful Correlations in Random Data.* Available: http://noosphere.princeton.edu/. Last accessed 24th June 2013.

- Foster Steven PHD, Little Meredith . (1984). The Medicine Name. In: Foster Steven PHD, Little Meredith *The Sacred Mountain*. Big Pine, CA: Lost Borders Press. p39.

- Browne Malcom . (1997). *Far Apart, 2 Particles Respond Faster Than Light.* Available: http://www.nytimes.com/1997/07/22/science/far-apart-2-particles-respond-faster-than-light.html. Last accessed 24th June 2013.

- Collins English Dictionary- Complete & Unabridged 10th Edition. (2013). *inquiry.* Available: http://dictionary.reference.com/browse/inquiry?s =t:. Last accessed 25th June 2013.

- Corvalan Carlos ,Hale Simons, McMichael Anthony. (2005). Ecosystems and human well-being : health synthesis . In: José Sarukhán ... [et al.] *A report of the Millennium Ecosystem Assessment,* Geneva: http://www.who.int/entity/globalchange/ecosystems/ecosys.pdf. p6

- Enculescu Silvana. (2012). *Austerity and euro crisis see suicides increase* . Available: http://www.publicserviceeurope.com/article/2479/get-serious-about-combating-suicide-europe-urged.. Last accessed 17th June 2013.

- Institute of HeartMath, (2012). The Heartmath Definition . *Newsletter Summer 2012 http://www.heartmath.org/templates/ihm /e-newsletter/publication/2012/summer/heartmath-definition.php /.* Vol.11 / No.2 (2), p1

- Mahmood Moazam ,Lee Woori .(2013). Macroeconomic challenges have worsened. *Global Employment Trends 2013/ International Labour Organization/ 2013/ISBN 978-92-2-126656-3 (pdf)* . 3 (2), p 15.

- Marcus Marina, YasamyTaghi, van Ommeren Mark, Chisholm, Dan, Saxena Shekhar. (2012). *Depression.* Available: http://www.who.int/mental_health/management /depression/who_paper_depression_wfmh_2012. pdf. . Last accessed 24th June 2013.

- Merriam-Webster . (2013). *Greed .[website]* Available: http://www.merriam-webster.com/dictionary/greed. Last accessed 24th June 2013.

- United Nations Department of Economics and Social Affairs (2012). *Millennium Development Goals Report 2012* . New York: United Nations http://www.un.org/en/development/desa/publicat ions/mdg-report-2012.html/. p6-28.

- Venefica Avia. (2012). *Symbolic meanings of The Raven In Native American Indian Lore.* Available: http://www.symbolic-meanings.com/2007/11/15/symbolic-meaning-of-the-raven-in-native-american-indian-lore. Last accessed 24th June 2013.

- World Health Organisation. (2015). *Mental HealthSuicide prevention (SUPRE/*. Available: http://www.who.int/mental_health/prevention/suicide/. Last accessed 29/12/2015

Printed in Great Britain
by Amazon